A Dream of Eden

The Dales of the Lake District
in Words and Pictures

Track by side of Watendlath Tarn. Pollarded ashes

A Dream of Eden

THE DALES OF THE LAKE DISTRICT IN WORDS AND PICTURES

Text by John Dawson

Photographs by David Briggs

CICERONE PRESS

ISBN 1 85284 104 4

British Library Cataloguing-in-Publication Data.
A catalogue record for this book is available from the British Library.

DEDICATIONS

The text of this book is dedicated by the author to Margaret
and the family; the photographs are dedicated by the
photographer to Jill, Sarah and Jenny.

CONTENTS

INTRODUCTION

IT WAS Wordsworth who first compared the dales of the Lake District to the spokes of a wheel, radiating from a hub appropriately situated, in, or near, Grasmere. Taking our cue from him, David Briggs and I have started from that hub, and threaded our way along the spokes, from valley to valley. We have not followed him, or anyone else, slavishly, although he turned out to be inescapable, and figures briefly, sometimes unexpectedly, in various chapters. We have concentrated our attention on the valleys, because they are the places where the people live, and if it were not for the work of the dalesfolk over many generations, the Lake District would not be the *dream of Eden* (to use a phrase of Mrs Linton) that we see today.

The present appearance of the dales no less than that of the high fells is the result of how human beings have interacted with the environment ever since Stone Age times, partly by exploiting it, partly by co-operating with it. We felt that there was a need for a book which looked specifically at the dales. The mountains cannot be ignored in doing this, but our paths have taken us through the settlements by the lakes and rivers. We have avoided main roads, except where they provide the most satisfactory access to a place, or, occasionally, the best viewpoint. As David's photographs show, some of the finest perspectives of the fells are from round their feet. Often there are several byways to follow through a particular valley, and we have not attempted to list all the possibilities. The scope for a person equipped with an O.S. map is endless, and it is all the more rewarding when a path has been discovered personally. So we have not set out defined ways, field by field, and stile by stile; nor have we spent time looking at the most obvious or best-known features of the valleys.

This book, then, is not a detailed gazetteer, taking the sparkle and romance out of the dales by listing every place in a charmless monotone. It is our impression of the Lake District, not as the result of a short note-taking tour, but built up over many years. We live here, and have been able to get to know some of the dalesfolk. We have looked at their daily lives, and focused on those aspects of their work and leisure pursuits that make this area different from anywhere else in the world. Nor are these lives just a background to a million hiking or touring holidays; they are the process through which the landscape that we have inherited is being passed on, subtly transformed, to our successors. To achieve the object we have set ourselves, we have tried not to be either patronising or prying; after all, we ourselves are part of the scene we are describing. Our own outlook and attitudes have been shaped through long contact with our neighbours.

In the preparation and presentation of the book, we have formed a partnership. This is neither a written 'guide', illustrated by photographs, nor a collection of photographs, strung together by a text. Written word and image complement each other. David's photographs depict the landscape and the people going about the business of their lives with an immediacy and effect that even the pen of a Ruskin or a Wordsworth could never match: the text sometimes ranges over incidents and activities which it would be impossible to photograph. The nearest parallel in our book is perhaps the one which the Lintons produced in the mid-1860s while they were living at Brantwood. William's delightful wood engravings complement Eliza's forceful text in a volume which, like this one, is based on the real experience of living in the Lake District. As a tribute to their work, some of Mrs Linton's observations from their *Guide to the Lake Country* have been used as epigraphs to each of our chapters.

Today, there seems to be such a compulsive need to label everything, and parcel it out in neat manageable portions, to make everything plain even if this means reducing it all to the status of a moving peep show. On a cold morning last winter, the writer was standing in the street at Coniston, commiserating with an elderly lady on the state of her rheumatism, when a car that had passed us stopped abruptly. A young woman flourishing an enormous camera leapt out and accosted us: "Gee! You look so ENGLISH. I'd like to take a photograph of you!" Fortunately, the lady was as wryly amused as I was. We concluded that my Sherlock Holmes hat and knee breeches had triggered the incident that will enshrine us for ever as "Two Lake District Natives". David and I have tried to make our way more slowly into the life of the place; we have been willing to accept the inconsistencies and eccentricities, to marvel at the wonderful way in which the web of life is woven. Here, history and geography have combined to create something unique. We have attempted to catch the special flavour, and hope that our work may help others to understand more of the Lake Country, to see it in its context as the homeland of a busy and talented people.

Many of these people have helped us by talking freely about their work or their special interests, especially Margaret Atkinson, Wilfred Barker, Peter Cooper, Walter Dry, Alan Foster, Malcolm Grindrod, David Hawkes, John Hext, Jack Longmire, Allan Mason, Peter Martin, Elizabeth Prickett, Fred Reeves, Anthony Robinson, Keith Rowand, Don Shepherd, David Thompson, David and Gwen Williamson, Alan Wilson, Bunty Wilson and Robin Woodend. David would also like to thank all those who assisted him in the course of the photography.

In thanking them, the authors must point out that any errors which have crept into the text and the captions are our own responsibility! We must also thank Walt Unsworth and the staff of Cicerone Press for their help and encouragement in all the stages through which a book must pass from being an idea bandied over the table, to the finished volume on the shelf.

Churchyard gates, Grasmere

I: Grasmere and the Langdales

Of all the Lake Country villages, Grasmere is the most picturesque and the likest one's idea of the typical English home. It is full of flowers and green trees and pleasant meadows and lovely little lanes, and the signs of human care throughout.
Mrs Linton, 1864

OUR STARTING point, just about the centre of the Lake District, is one of Grasmere's less well-known landmarks - the stone drinking fountain and trough in the angle formed by the old road into the village and the newer by-pass. It was clearly architect-designed, no expense spared, in meticulously dressed stone which forms a neat little gable over a Norman arch decorated with the authentic dog-tooth pattern. The inscription on the gable reads *In Memory of Wordsworth*. There is no getting away from him either at Grasmere or in the entire Lake District, even if you deliberately start across the road with your back to Dove Cottage. But this fountain reminds us of something besides one of England's finest poets. It reminds us that for generations Grasmere has been a halting place on the main route through the Lakeland mountains; here the wayfarer and his horse would pause for refreshment before taking either the steep road past Dove Cottage and on towards Ambleside, or the long haul over Dunmail to Wythburn and points north.

A short walk into the village brings us to St. Oswald's Church, focal point of the community since at least the middle of the thirteenth century, when the earliest surviving records give Henry de Galdington as the rector of 'Grossmer'. This is how people whose roots are in the area still pronounce the name of the village, and inside the church we can feel something of that continuity which Wordsworth sensed so keenly and expressed so clearly. At first, when they brought the fresh rushes every August to strew the floor, there was simply the nave adjoining the plain and sturdy tower; but Grasmere parish included Langdale, Rydal and the northern end of Ambleside. When the population began to grow during the fifteenth century, the building became too small. The Langdale parishioners (no doubt as aware of their own separate identity then as they are today) took the initiative and pressed for an enlargement. In those days you didn't call in an architect at times like this. You gathered the men together and set to work. The simplest idea was to build another nave, on the north side of the existing one, then knock holes in the old wall to link the two together. Five big holes, in the form of rough arches. Maybe they even did this first, so as to be able to re-use the stone.

It wasn't long before they found that there was a serious drawback to the new design. Rain, snow and dead leaves in the gutter between the two roofs began to let water into the fabric of the building. But Langdale came to the rescue in 1562 when John Benson of Baisbrown - one of the principal farms in the valley - bequeathed money, *so that the roofe be taken down and made oop again.* Once more, they solved their problem pragmatically. They set another row of arches above the ones that now ran along the centre of the church. These supported the timbers for a new roof over the whole structure. The existing roof timbers they left in place, and there they remain. Although Langdale has long been a separate parish, that northern extension is still known as the Langdale aisle.

There is much more in the church to interest the visitor, but one feature relates directly to the life of the village today. On the central pillar to the left of the nave is a Madonna and Child sculpted by Ophelia Gordon Bell. She was the wife of W.Heaton Cooper, whose father, Alfred, was also a celebrated Lakeland painter. The third generation of this remarkable and talented family has maintained the tradition; over the years they have helped to make Grasmere the artistic centre of the Lake District.

Leaving the churchyard by the lychgate, we inevitably stop at the little old cottage where Sarah Nelson began to sell her special gingerbread well over a century ago. She was well placed strategically, because most of the tourists seeking to pay homage at Wordsworth's grave passed through this gate, and the delightful smell of freshly baked gingerbread brought them into the shop on their way out! The traditional recipe is still used, the same smell entices us inside to sample this unique amenity.

Dusting away the last treacly crumbs from our lips, we take the metalled road leading towards Red Bank. Soon a footpath guides us down to the quiet shore of the lake. Single huge alders follow the margin of the water. A flock of Canada geese is grazing in the adjoining field; others keep up-ending themselves in the shallow water, just as ducks do. Not a bit dignified, and what a contrast to the two swans posing near the reed beds on the opposite shore. Grasmere village is no longer visible, the ceaseless traffic on the main road is barely audible, and the only jarring note comes from a strident party of gulls chivvying a harmless picnic party for leftovers. A shallow weir across its outfall regulates the flow of water into the River Rothay. In the pool below are several ducks. The last member of the group is still on top of the weir; unusually adventurous, or not very bright, he shoots the rapids in a flurry of foam and feathers, then ostentatiously shakes the water from his wings as he joins his friends.

From this point, we may either take the low road, by the shore of Rydal Water, or go

Rowing boats awaiting the "visitors", Grasmere

by the higher way, from which there is a broader view back over the vale, up to Helm Crag, looking rather small, and Sergeant Man, a pimple on the mountain horizon. This higher path has the advantage that it leads the walker past some spectacular disused quarries. One presents a wide cavernous opening; inside, it is warm and still, except for the water dripping musically from the jagged rock that forms the roof. Along one wall runs a clear geological fault line, like the arch of a rainbow. From the spoil heap outside you can look across to the vertical crags on Nab Scar, picked out by the afternoon sun, and down on Rydal Water, with the two swans making a stately highlight near its head. (Do they have a duty rota? "It's our turn to sit on Rydal this afternoon, dear, yawn, yawn..." Or are they plastic, put there by the planning board?) A second quarry is wilder, more restless than the cavern - all sheer faces and jagged edges. Against the sky, a few feathery larches keep a toehold in the pitifully thin layer of dark soil spread over the rock like icing on a wedding cake. The intermittent splashes of water from the black recesses here are more sinister than musical.

The path now runs through woodland, golden yellow in autumn when the big old ashes are fading, to Pelter Bridge. From here the most convenient way to the Brathay Valley and Langdale is by the public highway under Loughrigg, then through Clappersgate to Skelwith Bridge. In order to avoid motor traffic it would be necessary to leave the valleys, and go over Loughrigg Fell - a superb short walk. Great Langdale effectively begins at Skelwith. A footpath runs through the quarry yard en route for Skelwith Force, where one must be prepared for anything. On a December afternoon in 1989 the rocks above the falls were bedizened with young people in bright blue or orange garments. They had rigged up a sort of washing line, by the aid of which they were perilously traversing the force.

That day provided a perfect illustration of the contrasting ways in which visitors and residents use the area. No sooner beyond the trees above the force, than from the fields across the river arose a terrible mingled shout of men and hounds, accompanied by the bray of a hunting horn. By the time it was possible to see the source of the hullabaloo, the excitement had subsided. Hounds were milling round aimlessly, merging into the winter shadows; two men with spades appeared to be burying something. As we went on to Elterwater they all began to drift back towards Skelwith.

Elterwater was frozen that afternoon, the distant mountains more than ever like sleeping giants - *great, unscaleable monsters* thought Mrs Linton. On such a day the river above the lake has clear, still reaches in which the trunks of the bankside trees are perfectly reflected, and each stone that forms the river bed is distinctly defined. Usually, of course, the water is anything but still, and roars down under the bridge at Elterwater village. From here one may go on to Chapel Stile by the road, or detour over the shoulder of Lingmoor, for the sake of the wider views and freedom from traffic. This route passes the youth hostel where, in days gone by, flax was dried on the lawn. From farther up the road, with Wetherlam looming above the mosaic of trees, it is possible to pick out Neaum Crag House, back near Skelwith.

There is a link between the flax on the lawn and the distant house. Albert Fleming, a prominent figure in the then fashionable Arts and Crafts Movement, lived at Neaum Crag during the late nineteenth century. He was a friend of John Ruskin, who, aware of the long tradition of flax growing in the area, was looking for a way to link this with some kind of cottage-based craft. He seems to have seen it as an additional source of income for

Reflections, Loughrigg Tarn

the cottagers, but Ruskin was stronger on the broad visionary sweep than the nitty-gritty details of real life. After one visit to Italy he brought back some drawings of reticella lace work which he had seen, and liked, in Venice. Could this sort of thing be done, using linen, perhaps linen made from flax grown in the fields next to the local cottages? What did Albert think of the possibilities?

No doubt in his mind's eye he saw them sitting outside their cottages, on sunlit summer evenings, plying their needles. Albert was courteous enough to take the drawings, and he showed them to his housekeeper, Marion Twelves, who was an accomplished needlewoman. This was the end of Ruskin's practical involvement, apart from giving Miss Twelves permission to use his name in connection with her work in 1894, after she had moved to Keswick. Meanwhile, Fleming provided what little organisation there was, and Marion worked out as best she could how to make the 'lace' by studying the drawings.

Almost single-handed, around the turn of the century, she popularised this new craft, first round Langdale and Coniston, then from her own base in Keswick. In Langdale, Mrs Pepper became the founder of a notable dynasty of lacemakers; in Coniston, Mrs Alan Coward even succeeded for a time in making Ruskin lace commercially. She operated a putting-out system, which was not in the least what Ruskin had envisaged, covering every process from spinning the flax and weaving the linen cloth to packing the ten-inch square place mats for despatch to Heal's or Liberty's, where they retailed at £5 for a set. They were an expensive prestige item, to enhance the dinner tables of the rich. But the demand faded away in the 1920s - these severely plain little pieces cut no ice with the swinging Art Deco generation, and antimacassars went out of fashion as men's hair styles changed. For years the continuing existence of the craft hung on a thread - a tiny group of enthusiasts kept it going until changed social conditions created a situation in which women (mainly) found themselves with the leisure to pursue a fascinating and creative hobby, that requires neither a great deal of space nor a big capital outlay.

The 'lace' is, in fact, a combination of drawn-thread and cut-linen work. To put it crudely, the worker cuts a square out of the fabric, then sets about filling the hole with a geometrical pattern of threads. The closely confined framework, and the monotone colour scheme provide a strictly disciplined framework, within which an endless variety of creative expression is possible. The final effect, whether a lampshade, a pincushion or even a wall-hanging is being made, depends on the skill with which the pattern has been built up in the squares. At the time of writing, a Ruskin lace class flourishes at Skelwith, under the guidance of Mrs Elizabeth Prickett of Torver, whose book on the subject is the standard work about this unusual craft.

Arriving at Chapel Stile, by whatever route, the walker is not likely to linger. Like Coniston, this is a small nineteenth century industrial centre onto which the tourist industry of the twentieth century has been grafted. Moreover, by this stage, Great Langdale beckons irresistibly. The best days are often in autumn or winter; a heart-stopping vision of dissolving cloud round the top of Harrison Stickle, and the low angle of the morning sun illuminating the architecture of the vast buttresses sweeping down to the valley floor. The cloud shadow above Stickle Tarn is heightened by the brightness of the sunlight. Yet even as you gaze, the cloud melts away, and every detail of the rock faces becomes clear, right to the summits. You can see this sort of thing better from the valley footpaths than when you are actually creeping up the mountainside. There is an admirable path through

Beech woods and bridge over the River Brathay

most of Langdale, which avoids the road. 'Admirable' is an adjective chosen with care. The problem with Langdale is the number of people who go there. Without very careful and sensitive management life would become intolerable for the residents, while the sheer number of visitors would destroy what they come to enjoy.

So there is just a feel about these paths that you are in a public park, slightly sanitised and discreetly managed, even on the rare days when there is hardly anyone about except the local sheep. The farms beyond Baisbrown are on the south-facing side of the valley; their land runs across its flat floor in front, and away up the fellside behind. The river is held brutally in place by great bastions of stone, which may or may not withstand the next calamitous run-off from those overwhelming mountains. Everything here is on the grand scale - the intimate little corners that we can see in Kentmere or Yewdale are hard for the visitor to find. The craggy outcrops fall right to the roadside, the valley bottom somehow seems almost as bare as it was when the glacier first levelled it.

On one of the accessible little crags, a group of young people is receiving basic training in rock work: perhaps the party which was trying to cross Skelwith Force on a rope. All great fun no doubt on a fine, sunny morning, but just another example of how so many folk now want to walk and climb on the mountains. Even careful training is no insurance against accident, and in Langdale the mountain rescue team has a great deal of work to do. The members of the Lakeland rescue teams are drawn from all walks of life, brought together by their common concern that no-one should be left injured or hopelessly lost out on the fells.

The call may come at any time - a quarryman may just have started his evening meal after a hard day's work. Hastily snatching another slice of bread while he reaches for his rucksack, always kept packed ready in the hall, he hurries to the assembly point. "A young chap," he is told, "above Stickle Tarn, somewhere. Broken leg, the police say. Should be pretty straightforward." The young man's companion had come racing down, and alerted the police by telephone from Dungeon Ghyll, where she was waiting for the rescuers to guide them back to the scene of the mishap. Meanwhile other team members have arrived, each one signing in - a wise precaution for insurance purposes, and in case one of the rescuers themselves should be missing at the end of the day.

By now the team's big Land Rover has set off with the advance party. They will unload the stretcher at the point where the vehicle can go no farther. Here, some will wait for the main party, while others go at once up the stony track, with first aid equipment and an emergency bag into which the victim can be placed if there is any risk of him being in danger from exposure. The different sections of the team keep in touch with each other and their base by radio; they will have power lights rather like portable car headlamps because their anxious guide, in her flustered excitement, might mistake the way, leaving dusk to fall before anyone has located her injured companion. Here the cumulative experience of the team members can be a big help in guessing the most likely spots where the accident could have taken place.

While all this is going on, the police will have arranged for an ambulance to be summoned to Dungeon Ghyll. The main body of the team will be needed to bring the loaded stretcher back: ideally eight men act as bearers, keeping the stretcher as horizontal as possible. They take half-hour turns on a long carry and, in the dark, need guidance from colleagues behind who are training power lights on the terrain ahead. If this is indeed a

Early morning mist on the River Crake

Yew Tree Farm, Yewdale

Elterwater village and the Langdale Pikes

straightforward rescue, the unfortunate young man will soon be delivered to the waiting ambulance. Team members now have to repack their equipment, and return to base before signing out and returning home to finish their meals. Older team members have been at the base the whole time to co-ordinate further help if necessary, or to pass on radio messages from the searchers.

If this is a simple rescue, a complicated one can be imagined only with difficulty. The young man might have fallen from one of the great rock faces - Dow Crag, maybe, over at Coniston - and be lying critically injured. Then the local team would send for the R.A.F. rescue helicopter. The machine can be on the scene almost in the time it takes for a small advance party to reach the sufferer, and can have him in hospital within an hour. The skill of the helicopter pilot in manoeuvring his craft as close as possible to the injured person is staggering - team members tell of the rotor blades circulating within inches of the precipice while the casualty is being transferred by rescuers. But in a way the worst rescue operation is when a person is lost, and no-one knows whether the object of the search is alive or dead. In this situation the rescue dogs can often provide vital information.

These dogs, which can be of any breed, as long as they are agile, sure-footed, intelligent and big enough to cover a lot of rough ground without tiring, work by air scent, and can even pick out a person who has been lying injured for a couple of days. Their handlers are often members of one or other of the rescue teams, and they will comb an area before the main body of human searchers arrives to distract them with a whole battalion of new scents. The handler has to have a lot of patience as well as an understanding of dogs. The training is rigorously organised by the Search and Rescue Dogs Association, and dogs which have passed their four-day examinations are re-tested at regular intervals.

Training starts by the handler leaving his dog with a friend, and going off to hide at a gradually increased distance. Next the dog has to look for another person - no doubt usually a long-suffering member of the handler's family - in all weather conditions, including snow. Finally the dog must learn to find strangers - willing friends of the handler - who have to go and lie up in some unfrequented spot. Since the work can often take place during the hours of darkness, the handler himself has to be very experienced in traversing difficult county under the worst possible conditions, because he carries the emergency first aid equipment. The dog carries, not a brandy flask, but a green light stick on his harness. This is about 20 millimetres thick and as long as a pencil, and gives out a glow which enables the handler to keep in touch more effectively and get to the scene if the dog indicates that he has found something by barking. The handler now has to unpack his first aid kit and radio back to rescue headquarters. At the end of the year this toilsome and hazardous day's work will appear in the S.A.R.D.A. equipment officer's report in such laconic wording as "So-and-so, working his two dogs, A and B, carried out initial search for climber missing, having set out to climb Bowfell Buttress. After a 2¼-hour search he was found by A unhurt, having been benighted on the buttress."

Walking on through Langdale, we eventually reach Stool End Farm, now the last one in the valley, just below the path which leads along the Band and so up to Bowfell. The sun doesn't spend a lot of time here in winter, but how different on a brilliant July afternoon! No-one thinks of searches and rescues then. The paths up Rossett Gill and to the pikes stand out like scars. Newly clipped Herdwick sheep are grazing in the field next to the farm, protected by walls of rounded cobbles, matched next to the farm buildings by

Right:
Chris Akrigg (Cockley Beck Farm, Duddon Valley) and George of Fell Foot Farm, Little Langdale, driving sheep down Greenburn for sorting and shearing at Fell Foot Farm

Left:
George hand-clipping a sheep at Fell Foot Farm, Little Langdale

a new wall in the same style. The tenant of this National Trust farm, Mr Keith Rowand, has not only renewed his walls but also built a new stock and general purpose building, faced with this same local stone and roofed with Lakeland slate. It blends perfectly with the old farmstead, and all merge into the landscape as if they had grown there. Looking into Mickleden beyond the farm, or into Oxendale on the other side of the Band, the green of the hay meadows soon gives way to a harsher pattern of browns. In Oxendale the valley floor is strewn with boulders from times when the beck has flooded. On the far slope is a fan of scree at the foot of a deep gully cut into the crag face. Not many yards beyond the gully another path climbs out of the valley, the work of the National Trust warden for this area and his team.

In order to reduce the fearful erosion caused by the trampling of so many boots and the annual fall of so many feet of rain the National Trust, helped by the Lake District Planning Board, is gradually creating carefully graded, well constructed footpaths along popular routes. They are made by traditional methods, using stone gathered from the nearby fellside. There are transverse cuts to allow drainage sikes to cross the line of the path, which has been given a solid permanent base by the stone pitching. Walking up is relatively easy, rather like a series of rough shallow steps, and big boulders define the edges. The team reinstates damaged ground along the route, by reseeding the eroded gullies that they have filled in. After laying the path, the team sees to its maintenance - keeping the transverse cuts clear, even sowing grass seed in the crevices between the stones. These paths make walking much easier, and they are far less obtrusive to the eye than the terrible lines that are being created where they do not exist. The only trouble is that there are far too few hands available to make the miles of path that ideally are needed.

The same considerations apply to the hundreds of miles of wall for which the National Trust is responsible. In the end work has to be restricted to essential features - like the superbly restored sheepfold in Oxendale, or old boundary walls, and the long stretches, sometimes called ring garths, which separate the better quality valley land from the rougher, partly wooded, lower slopes of the fells.

The way from Great Langdale to Yewdale crosses the hause by Blea Tarn into Little Langdale, a road sorely harassed by the stream of vehicles doing the Langdale round, or the Wrynose/Hardknott adventure run. But the pedestrian is able to take the quiet way on the far side of the valley and feel something of its special atmosphere. An elderly tractor, rusted by continual work through many seasons of Cumbrian rain, is spluttering across a steeply sloping field.

These Lakeland dales are the daily workplace for those who farm the land. In spring the grass has been cropped as short as a cricket outfield, where the sheep have been trying to find an early bite. A little later in the year these same fields will be loud with the cry of lambs. Near one of the farms a girl may perhaps be seen persuading a bewildered ewe to accept an orphan lamb. The ewe has lost her own lamb, and its skin has been tied round the pathetic scrap of wool that is nuzzling at her teat. By July the grass will have grown enough to be cut for hay, filling the summer air with its fragrance.

Later still, the walker may meet a shepherd setting out with his dogs to gather the sheep that have been grazing the high summer pastures. The Fell Foot shepherd in Little Langdale works with his opposite number at Cockley Beck, the last farm at the head of Dunnerdale. Keith Rowand from Stool End has an amicable fell top frontier with the shepherds from upper Eskdale. In the course of a working day the hill shepherd will outwalk any but the hardiest holidaymaker, and then get to work in the sheep pens after a short break for his 'bait'.

Long ago the Roman legionaries marched through Little Langdale on their way from Ambleside to Ravenglass. No-one has been able to satisfactorily define the line of their road, but even the casual passer-by cannot miss the haunted ruins of long abandoned farms, and the wrecks of what were once busy quarries. Walkers may still use the old Slaters' Bridge down near the ford from which the road meanders up to Stang End. From here, now in more enclosed, wooded country, littered with abandoned slate quarries, there are several ways across to Yewdale. The most direct is to go almost to Hodge Close, then to continue past High Oxenfell. A short diversion at Hodge Close enables us to peer into the most spectacular ruined quarry of them all - sheer slabs of smooth slate hurtling into the flooded quarry floor. Visitors flock here to learn abseiling on these vertical faces or to fossick in the water, wearing their wetsuits and snorkels.

The discriminating walker will savour the upland road past High Oxenfell. It has all the features of a Lakeland landscape to perfection; uneven brackeny heathland; irregularly shaped stone-walled green fields; patches of old woodland, and a distant prospect of big mountains. From Yewdale top we shall gradually be leaving those mountains behind.

Woodland, Yewdale

II: Yewdale and the Crake Valley

Over by Oxenfell and Yewdale runs the beautiful fellside road; one of the richest, the most varied, and the most picturesque; well worthy to be known and loved by all who care for the noblest kind of hill-side scenery.

Mrs Linton.

JOHN RUSKIN could see Yewdale and its crags from his home at Brantwood, and he quickly became aware of its unusually attractive character. As early as 1872 he wrote, in the collection of public letters which he issued under the title *Fors Clavigera (No.XV): Last autumn I saw, even in modern England, something bright; low sunshine at 7 o'clock of an October morning, glancing down a long bank of fern covered with hoar frost, in Yewdale, at the head of Coniston Water. I noted it as more beautiful than anything I had ever seen, to my remembrance, in gladness and infinitude of light.*

The intimate scale of the somehow friendly atmosphere of this valley, contrasting with the steep crags that form its western wall, captivated the old philosopher as surely as they captivate us today. His private diaries record how he loved to walk its quiet byways to special little places for which he had a particular affection - as on April 14, 1883 when he took Kate Greenaway *up Yewdale stream, and showed her the white rose tree on the roof of the cottage by the brook.*

It is still possible to walk the whole length of Yewdale with scarcely more than a step on the busy motor road and, though the white rose tree has gone, each of us can find our own corner of Eden here. Even on a cold winter day the path down to High Yewdale is sheltered by trees. Ice tinkles beneath the boot, a wren flies up from the little wooden bridge over the stream. The road below is completely blocked by two Land Rovers, side by side, but there is no need to worry; it is just a couple of farmers passing the time of day. The sunlight that so moved Ruskin is illuminating the tops of the larches above the little tarn, known locally as Marshall's Tarn, or T'fish Tarn. It is an artificial tarn, like Tarn Hows as we see it today, created by the Marshall family who lived at Monk Coniston for several generations from the mid-nineteenth century, and who were responsible for much of the imaginative tree planting that has enriched this part of the Lake District. On this frosty morning the sheltered field below the dam at the outlet of the tarn is white with hoar frost, except for little green patches where the sheep have been lying during the night.

A field path opposite High Yewdale Farm runs alongside the famous line of yew trees to Low Yewdale. For many years there was a formal garden, adorned by elaborate topiary work, in front of High Yewdale and, according to local tradition, the yews date from this period, each one commemorating the birth of a child in the family! Nearer to Low Yewdale there is an outcrop of Coniston Limestone. The ridge, crowned with trees, crosses the valley floor to the big limekiln situated near the road. This narrow band of limestone is the marker separating the fierce volcanic angles of the crags from the quieter landscape of Silurian rock which gives lower Yewdale its more pastoral charm. The walker can remain on the Silurian side of the divide all the way to Coniston.

The track runs through more woodland before emerging near a stand of big yews, fenced for the protection of stock. Through the smoky sunlight which helps to conceal the village, the lake shines in a silver line. Closer to hand, the dark mass of the yews contrasts with the delicate textures of larch and birch against the pale winter sky. The silence is complete until a distant chain saw begins to whine and, somewhere among the trees, a woodpecker laughs. Old Man and Wetherlam form an alpine background to the nearer crags that Ruskin felt were, so to speak, staring him in the face whenever he looked from his study window.

The mountain panorama from Brantwood, he claimed, was one of the finest to be seen anywhere - and he was more familiar with the Alps than most people. A century earlier, Thomas West, one of the pioneers of Lakeland discovery, described the wonders of the view from the middle of the lake in terms which now seem grotesquely exaggerated: *the finest exhibition of rural elegance (cultivation and pasturage, waving woods and sloping inclosures, adorned by nature, and improved by art) under the bold sides of stupendous mountains, whose airy summits the elevated eye cannot now reach, and which almost deny access to the human kind.* The obvious course is to go and see for ourselves.

A few minutes from the viewpoint by the yew trees bring us into Coniston village, a small nineteenth century boom town created by the exploitation of the copper mines, and subsequently improved and adorned by the twentieth century tourist industry. West's station on the water is not an option in the winter, but for the rest of the year, Coniston's celebrated pleasure boat awaits us at the foot of Lake Road. Alternatively, we may emulate Ruskin, who habitually used his rowing boat to get to and from the village. For example, on June 30, 1883, when he was in his mid-sixties" *I not fatigued, though rowing with Eliot* (Charles Eliot Norton, a friend) *to and fro the Waterhead. Tea (with the Marshalls) at Monk Coniston. Unsatisfactory.*

We may be quite certain that to sail with S.Y.Gondola will not be fatiguing, either; and that the total experience will be satisfactory. Brantwood is immediately visible on the eastern shore, a big rambling Victorian house, whose gardens in early summer are aflame with masses of rhododendrons and azaleas. The woods behind consist mainly of oak, with areas given over to hazel coppice. These now neglected coppice woods are a relic of the days when High Furness was an industrial region. Every fifteen years or so the hazel poles would be cut down to their base or stool, to be used by the charcoal burners who figure so picturesquely in some of Arthur Ransome's books. The circular pitsteads, level platforms about fifteen feet in diameter, where the charcoal fires burned may be easily identified by a person walking in the woods. Nearer the foot of the lake the land becomes more open. Meadows line the shore towards Water Park, and there are extensive reed beds where the River Crake glides unobtrusively out of the lake to begin its short but tempestuous journey to the sea at Greenodd.

These reed beds are a delight to ornithologists and to pike fishermen. Arthur Ransome tells in his autobiography how he and his father fished here, whistling to their spaniel on the bank so that it would splash through the reeds and drive the pike out into more open water. There are also the remains of quays at the foot of the lake where, in the old days, all manner of heavy goods were unloaded to be taken down the valley by cart or packhorse: often it would be slate or copper from Coniston or gunpowder from Elterwater. A little building, rather apart from the rest of the hamlet of High Nibthwaite, is still known as the 'gunpowder barn', where the stuff was stored overnight when necessary. On the return journey the boats would take saltpetre for the gunpowder works and bulky commodities like lime or charcoal.

As Gondola continues her circuit, we can see that the western shore of the lake is rougher and wilder than the eastern side. Some of the old woodland remains here, as well as traces of forgotten industries such as the iron smelting 'bloomeries' where ore from Low Furness was heated by means of the abundant local charcoal to make crude lumps or 'blooms' of iron. The bloomery sites may be recognised by the scatter of cindery slag mixed with the stones at the lake edge in a number of places. Nearing Coniston again, we sail close by Coniston Hall, home of the Fleming family for centuries, and now owned by the National Trust. The great banqueting hall, refitted by the Flemings in the reign of Elizabeth I, has undergone a second refit in the reign of Elizabeth II, and the massive cylindrical chimneys, so characteristic of the oldest manor houses in Furness, have been repaired and stabilised.

The northern part of the lake is very busy during the holiday season, so Gondola has to pick a careful way among shoals of canoes, dinghies and sailboards. In fact, so many people, not all of them experienced, use the lake for recreation that the presence of a rescue launch is far from being an over-protective luxury. There may also be a few fishermen about, because Coniston Water has always been famous for its fishing. Sir Daniel, a particularly formidable Fleming, writing in the 1680s observed that: *the fishing of Coniston Water hath time out of mind belonged to the Lords of Coniston aforesaid (i.e. his own family)...* and that *in the lake are yearly got with nets many pikes, or jacks, bass or perch, trouts, eels and charrs, which last is a kind of fish that is much esteemed and valued.*

Succeeding generations have endorsed Sir Daniel's judgement on the char, a smallish fish rather like an unusually delicate trout in appearance and flavour. These days the catch is not what it was, due to overfishing and a combination of ecological factors, but Coniston

Holme Ground Tarn, Tilberthwaite

remains one of the two lakes (the other is Windermere) specially associated with the fish. The traditional char fisherman will be out early in the morning in his rowing boat. He has two long rods - ash poles, very likely, set at right angles from the boat. At the end of each rod is a little bell. Once the boat has been rowed to deeper water, it is time to let down the line from each rod - twelve to fifteen fathoms of it, pulled down by a heavy lead weight. The line is festooned with a number of bright, home-made spinners, of gold, silver, brass or copper. (They used to say wedding rings were especially well suited to this employment.)

The line has to be so long because during the season (summertime, broadly) the char are to be found in shoals in the colder depths of the lake. The spinners presumably attract the fish by their brightness, or annoy them to the extent that they attack them, because they bear no resemblance to the char's normal diet. (But then, do salmon ever eat real flies?) Often men fish for char in pairs. One will guide the boat gently up and down, while the other attends to the lines. Soon one of the bells will tinkle through an unseen pull far below. When the line has been hauled in far enough to bring the fish to the surface, a net is dextrously swept under the splashing victim. All that remains is to disengage the fish from the spinner; by the time the line has been let down again, the other bell could easily be ringing. On a good day a pair of experienced fishermen will bring homes scores of fish. They used to make them into potted char - so great a delicacy that the eighteenth century Furness ironmaster would send it to favoured customers - but nowadays everything goes straight into the freezer.

We disembark from Gondola at the pier by the mouth of Church Beck. A few yards to the north, at the mouth of Yewdale Beck, is Pier Cottage, celebrated for its association with Coniston's most famous boat, Bluebird, or rather Bluebirds, for the partnership of the Campbells, father and son, with Coniston, lasted for thirty-five years. When he raised his own world speed record to 141.74mph in August 1939, Malcolm was already an internationally famous figure, who had been establishing land speed records since 1924. It was only after he had passed the 300mph barrier at Bonneville Salt Flats, Utah, in 1935, that he turned his mind seriously to speed on the water. His first records in this element date from 1937 on Lake Maggiore, before he came to Coniston two years later. His son Donald, by then a young man, was already deeply involved emotionally in his father's obsession.

After the war Malcolm, despite failing health, resumed his activities in the Lake District, this time with a jet engine in his Bluebird. There were serious technical problems which even the legendary Leo Villa, the engineering wizard behind the scenes, had difficulty in overcoming. Then, before everything had been ironed out, Sir Malcolm died. This was the critical moment for Donald - but with hindsight we can see that he could do no other than carry on where his father had left off, even though he had never driven a Bluebird either on water or land. The first attempt was frustrated by an oil leak but after that Donald, with Leo Villa at his side, never looked back. He became a regular feature of Coniston life, with his headquarters at the Black Bull hotel, then at the Sun. He was a much more approachable man than his father, and became genuinely popular in the village. Photographs show him taking part in all kinds of activities; celebrating with the hotel staff; helping to clear up at the Black Bull after the disastrous flood of 1950; chatting to a group of soldiers who had come to gape at Bluebird, as did many thousands of other sightseers. There was often a crowd by the slipway at Pier Cottage; the guest houses were

Tarn Hows

always full when a record attempt was in prospect. Householders tell how they were approached by the hotel proprietors to accommodate additional visitors in any spare beds they could muster.

During the 1950s Donald edged up the record breaking speed in successive visits to Coniston - from 225.63mph in 1956 to 260.30mph in 1959. Each time the entire local community was willing him to succeed. The atmosphere was rather like that in a town whose football team has got to Wembley for a cup final. It was in 1964 that Donald reached his apogee when, in Australia, he broke both the world land and water speed records in the same calendar year. By this time the technology which had created problems when the first jet engine was installed at Coniston had advanced further to bring a new situation again. At speeds approaching 300mph the difficulty was keeping the boat in contact with the water. In fact the whole question arose, when does a boat cease to be a boat? Bluebird K7 probably moved as fast as it was possible to move for a machine that is still recognisably a boat, rather than a wingless aeroplane ingloriously denied its proper element. When Donald plunged back into the water on January 4, 1967 there was a terrible sense of a final dénouement in the village. In a way it was entirely appropriate that he should have gone in this manner, and anyone who comes along now trying to find his body does so at their peril. He has joined the select band of folk heroes like Scott and Hillary who attempted one of the ultimate challenges that a man can face.

History has not been kind to Coniston. Bluebird has flown; the ripples of vicarious fame created by the physical presence of John Ruskin have faded; the mines have become a hunting ground for industrial archaeologists; the railway has been dismantled; only one slate quarry remains active. Yet the tepid and condescending praise which the old guidebooks used to bestow on the village has come to seem less and less relevant. The industries may have gone, the captains and the kings may have departed, but the geography remains. No other Lakeland village enjoys the simultaneous benefits of three distinct kinds of scenery in its immediate neighbourhood - the incomparable parkland around the head of the lake, the lake itself, so accessible and so much a part of the historic genius of the place; and the huge protecting presence of Old Man. Scarred and pitted by centuries of quarrying and mining, eroded by the feet of millions of pilgrims toiling to the summit, yet indestructible, it seems the mountain has a more than symbolic or emotional link with the community at its foot, and no-one can live in Coniston for long without feeling its special and determining influence.

In sharp contrast the Crake Valley, running down to the sea at Greenodd, seems quiet and pastoral. Water Park, by High Nibthwaite at the foot of the lake, was once a monastic grange or herd-wick, when the monks of Furness Abbey held all the land on the east side of this valley, right up to Monk Coniston at the head of the lake - hence of course, the name, to distinguish it from Church Coniston, where the village was situated. You would never guess that in its time Nibthwaite has been a small industrial centre. There was even an ironworks here, and a track leading up into the woods is Coal Lane. Charcoal Lane, that is; the men who made the charcoal were known as colliers. Arthur Ransome was on good terms with them. They would put a number of clay pipes into a burn then leave them nicely blackened, ready for a cool smoke, at the Red Lion, Lowick Bridge, for him to pick up. The sole representative of this industrial tradition in 1991 is Owen Jones, a young man who has taken up the ancient craft of swill basket making with conspicuous skill.

Coniston Water from Nibthwaite

Below Nibthwaite green pastures slope gently towards the river, flowing swiftly but not noisily. The field hedges, except where they have been mutilated along the roadside by blunt flail cutters, are properly laid. Autumn is a wonderful season for places like this because there is such an abundant natural harvest waiting to be gathered - sloes, blackberries, rosehips, crab apples, hazel nuts and conkers. In the little garth by any of the farms there may be damsons too. And the variety of habitats within a small compass ensures a remarkable richness of bird life: 118 species have been recorded by Mr Leonard Cowcill of High Nibthwaite, ranging from the buzzards that wheel over the moor above to the kingfishers by the river. Not that the kingfishers have been enjoying a happy time in recent years, with mink infesting the river banks and canoeists the stream itself in ever-increasing numbers.

Across the valley from Nibthwaite is Blawith (pronounced Blaaath) where the church was built. Everyone else in the valley used to poke fun at Blawith, whether there was any justification or not. When they decided to erect a new steeple for the church, to house a bell in 1781, it seemed reasonable to sell off a piece of the heathery, rocky common above the village to raise the necessary cash. It was too good an opportunity to be missed. Ever since, the jeering doggerel of the neighbours has been remembered:

> Blawith poor people
> An auld church and a new steeple
> As poor as hell
> They had to sell
> A bit of fell
> To buy a bell
> Blawith poor people.

Lowick, surrounded by good farmland, where the roads are spattered with cow muck during the summer, is the central settlement of the Crake Valley, even more scattered than the others perhaps, but with a strong sense of its own identity, nowhere illustrated better than by its annual show, held on the first Saturday in September. Locally known as 'T'lile Royal', Lowick Show is the shop window for the valley farmers, craft workers and housewives. In the excitement of the competitive outdoor events or the glamour of the show ring, it is easy to overlook the importance of the 'produce' tent, supported principally by these ladies. Some of them will have been working with today in mind for many months.

The serious exhibitor will be up early on the day of the show. She may have between twelve and twenty separate items to pack carefully in her car before travelling to the showfield for nine o'clock. With luck, the morning will be fine, so there will be no problem getting everything inside the tent. But then each piece, displaying the show label, has to be placed in its proper section. Not all shows are as well mounted as Lowick, so the experienced exhibitor will have brought an emergency supply of paper plates, doilies and safety pins; and she will be prepared to stand up for herself if the space allocated to a particular class is unduly restricted. There will be no time to run an eye over the other competitors' entries - by ten o'clock the tent will be cleared to allow the judges and their stewards to begin work. By now, however, the exhibitors are glad to subside on the forms in the refreshment tent, or anywhere, and have a cup of coffee and a bite to eat. The rest of the morning is theirs - to watch the stock judging, or to gossip with friends and rivals.

As soon as the judging is over they are all back in the big marquee, looking first to see

Top left;
Christine Sutcliffe and Margaret
Harrison judge the fruit cakes at
Lowick Show

Centre left:
Owen Jones, swiller

Below:
Bob Saunders plucking the last
turkey, Christmas 1989

what prizes they have won, then to see how everyone else has done and to evaluate the performance of the judges: "See, all those cakes have been cut, but thay haven't all been tasted!" The canny judge will try to make it as obvious as possible that she has followed all the canons of careful judging. She will have pulled the scones apart across the middle to check their texture, tasted to see whether there is a suspicion of egg in a plain scone. The judge will also make sure that details of presentation are meticulously observed. She will leave knitted garments turned to show that she has looked not just at the evenness, but also at the finish of the seams. She will not award a first to a jar of jam, however good it tastes, unless the jar is very clean, well filled, has a transparent or new screw-top lid, and a neat label two-thirds of the way up the side giving the date and kind. The wily exhibitor naturally always tries to be a jump ahead of the judge. Currants are the best bet for fruit scones, because sultanas are liable to stick out of the mixture and burn in cooking. Pots of jam made earlier in the summer will have been examined, and the one or two with the fruit most evenly distributed put aside for showing.

There is a tremendous interest in the Lakeland shows, and competitors will often travel a long way to take part. (Lowick is unusual in that entry is restricted to the valley.) The prize money is certainly not the attraction - more the genuine regard which everyone has for the woman who can make these homely things efficiently and attractively. (The word 'woman' has to be used because, except in the wine making and honey classes, men, alas, seldom figure!) The classes, too, are interesting in the way they precisely reflect the real life of the dales. They are all things which the people who live here actually wear or eat as a matter of course. If a class does encourage something fancy, it is unlikely to be well supported - though one reason for this may be the problem of getting a fancy exhibit to the show tent in one piece: butter icing, for example, is a very fragile commodity.

And so, at a set time, the exhibitors are allowed to remove their entries. Like a plague of locusts they descend, and within minutes the whole wonderful display of domestic arts and skills has vanished. Or usually. Should you be thinking of taking part for the first time, don't bring your entries in a cardboard box and leave it on the wet grass under the trestle tables all day. If you do, as you emerge through the tent flap clutching your bulky box you will very likely find your eggs, saucers, buns and fruit cake rolling across the mud at your feet. And the moral of that, as the Duchess said to Alice, is always take some plastic bags.

A little nearer to the sea than Lowick is Spark Bridge. The name reflects the frankly industrial origin of the place. There was a big iron forge here from about 1710 until 1850. The steeper fall of the river below the dripping woods that overshadow the fern-hung walls made it feasible to harness the power of the water. A bobbin mill occupied the site from 1850 until recent times. The present day conversion of the mill into small houses reflects the transformation of Spark Bridge into a mixture of holiday houses, retirement homes and dormitory outposts of Ulverston and Barrow.

A short distance below Spark Bridge is Penny Bridge, where the River Crake becomes tidal. Penny Bridge itself is indistinguishable to passing visitors from Greenodd, but there is a frontier along the beck that runs down past the school. The name derives from the Penny family, who occupied the hall for generations. At Greenodd the agricultural odour that has followed us all the way from Nibthwaite gives way to the smell of the sea. It is situated at the confluence of two rivers - the Crake and the Leven from Windermere - and is the highest point of their common estuary which vessels could conveniently reach. There

Great Gable dominates the head of Wasdale

Grasmoor and Crummock Water

is no trace now of the quays where slate, iron or gunpowder used to be loaded. The village street is now stopped off to allow the A590 to run unimpeded to Barrow: formerly it continued right to the shore and Greenodd had all the racy character of a true port. The Ship Inn still keeps a sailing vessel on its sign as a reminder of past times. Tradition tells how groups of sailors would amuse themselves trying to hold on to the greased tail of a lively pig; and how a ship laden with coal once misjudged the tide, and coming in under sail ran her bowsprit through the window of one of the numerous beer houses.

Anglers occupy the site of the quays now because the line of the main channel runs close under the road embankment. If they have time to spare from winding in their reels or throwing out mighty casts, they can enjoy the prospect over the sands to the low wooded hills across the bay or watch the movements of the wading birds. From the view here, a person might well be in, say, Cornwall, but climb above the main street of Penny Bridge and look inland. There are the mountains we left behind at Nibthwaite, and to which we may most easily return by taking the main road from Greenodd over Gawthwaite moor, then through Grizebeck and Broughton to Duddon Bridge.

Duddon Bridge Iron Furnace - drystone wall!

III: Dunnerdale

(From a point above Ulpha Kirk.) *A marvellously beautiful view, turn where you will; to the richness of the open valley and the sea; to the white track of river; to the sterner distance before you, or the desolateness of the hillside, too bleak for cultivation and too poor for human life.*

Mrs Linton.

DUDDON BRIDGE is the point on the river below which the flat estuarine land broadens into the wide expanse of Duddon Sands. The stream here is usually shallow, its pebbly bed ideal for the holidaymakers who come to splash about on hot summer days. But on this March morning there are no bathers. A solitary man is untying his fishing rod from the roof of his car; out of the wooden pens below the road the acrid smell of sheep dip rises through the damp air. Upstream, where the angler is now making his way, the river is tree-lined. The steep hillside on what used to be the Cumberland side of Duddon, thickly covered with mixed woodland, cuts off the growing brightness that is coming in from the sea. Hidden within this dark woodland is one of the most important and best preserved sites of early industrial archaeology, the Duddon iron furnace.

During the 1980s the Planning Board undertook the consolidation of the extensive buildings to prevent them from deteriorating further, and it is now possible to see the furnace as it was during the last years of its working life in the 1860s. The furnace itself is on the lowest part of the site, so that a workman could transport the ore over a long ramp to tip it into the circular furnace mouth. Thirty feet below is the hearth, 8 foot 6 inches wide, lined with fire brick. The molten metal was channelled to a sow and pigs in the ground outside. A water-wheel at the back of the furnace tower operated a pair of giant bellows. Cams on the axle of the wheel made them rise and fall in turn, so that as one filled with air, the other emptied itself forcefully into the furnace. The haematite store is a little higher up the hillside. Now used as a general store building by the Board, its internal walls are still red-stained. Higher again is the huge main charcoal store. This is 100 foot in length, and as high as a church. It is built into the slope of the land, enabling loads of charcoal from the packhorses to be tipped through openings at ground level on the top side and taken out later from the wide doorways on the opposite side, below.

If Duddon Bridge furnace illustrates the strand of industrial enterprise which ran all the way up this valley, Duddon Hall, a little farther up the river and still on the Cumberland side, represents the pre-industrial gentry who used to dominate the area. It is an elegantly proportioned building, looking across parkland to the river, and has all the usual amenities of a Georgian mansion, including an ice house and a remarkable temple-like structure, a cross between a folly and a chapel. To what god, if any, the place was dedicated is by no means clear. Tradition asserts that in the later years of the eighteenth century Major John Cooper (who had been responsible for rebuilding the house, and for changing its name to Duddon Grove from the much more authentically local one of Whae Hoose) used to bring his sporting friends here on Sunday afternoons. Then they would make a circle with the 'pews' and settle down to a session of cockfighting.

This so-called 'sport' certainly commanded a wide following in the Lakeland valleys. The outline of a long-abandoned cockpit can be traced above many villages - Coniston, for example, and Torver. There were even facilities farther afield in such unexpected places as Rose Castle, now the residence of the Bishop of Carlisle, and the old Angel Hotel in Kendal. The *Westmorland Gazette* in April 1839 carried a very high-toned paragraph deploring an event which had *gone off* on Easter Saturday in the Rusland Valley. It had been *an assemblage of idle fellows* and was *an amusement which clasps in its foul and contaminating embrace alike the deeds of gaming, drunkenness and every consequent tendency.* Yet almost fifty years later, the President of the Cumberland and Westmorland Antiquarian and Archaeological Society could read a paper to members, which took for granted that everyone knew that the activity, though long since made illegal, continued.

It had such a long and respectable ancestry, for one thing, that matched awkwardly with the *Westmorland Gazette's* strictures. Cockpits were often in, or adjacent to, churchyards. At Alston, the prize for the winner of the mains on Shrove Tuesday was a prayer book. At many places on this same day, Carlisle and Wreay for example, schoolboys barricaded their school against the master. The not always good-natured proceedings which followed concluded with high festival - cakes and ale, a football match and a cockfight. At Wreay the prize for the winner of this was a small silver bell.

At most cockpits the cocks were required to fight in 'fair silver spurs'. The spur was a spike of silver, slightly curved, about 1½ inches long. It had a ring to fit on the stump of the natural spur, and a leather to be lashed round the bird's leg. In a fight a good gamecock would seize his foe by the hackle, hold him down, and spur him on the head - so a spur had to be set very carefully, lest the cock should mutilate himself. This point about the actual combat explains why a further requirement was that cocks were to fight 'with a fair hackle' - that is, not trimmed away so that there was no hold for an adversary. The sharp silver spur was not a refinement of cruelty; it either killed at once or inflicted clean wounds which soon healed. The natural spur, being less sharp, caused bruise wounds which healed only slowly or led to a lingering death.

Chancellor Ferguson, from whose paper these details are taken, quoted from a letter in which one of the 'gentlemen of the sod', as cockfighting buffs were known, described details of the preparation for a fight: *Now these cocks were taken from their walks say, today, Friday, and fought about Monday or Tuesday week... On the first part of their training was cut a little of their wings and tail, then Senna tea to drink until, say, Tuesday, cut their spurs short and spar them every day, with small boxing gloves tied to their heels. On Tuesday they get their medicine - the very best Turkey rhubarb and magnesia, about the thickness of your first finger, in fact more than would quickly operate on you or me; next day Senna tea again and sparring. They get very much reduced by Friday, all the fat out of them - after that they give them new milk and bread made of eggs, loaf sugar etc., in fact everything that is good, the very best malt barley and so on - you would be astounded how they thrive each day after...*

Fifty years later still, in 1938, there were several convictions for cockfighting in Westmorland, and Doreen Wallace in her book *English Lakeland* (Batsford, 1940) describes how a gamecock belonging to a friend (she lived in Lorton village at the time) *stalked 500 yards up the road, and slew our domestic chanticleer, who had unwisely crowed in the still of the morning, but was otherwise guiltless.* Fifty years on again, and cockfighting has surely joined bull-baiting and riding the stang in Lakeland history.

Leaving Duddon Hall to the ghosts of its turbulent past, and the angler to the peaceful enjoyment of his pastime, we follow the road up the hill, turning off at the open fell along the byway to Beckstones. From here a bridle path runs through Ulpha Park past Frith Hall to rejoin the hill road below Old Hall. From the more commonly used road into the Duddon Valley on the Lancashire side of the river, Frith Hall is easily mistaken for the ruins of a castle seen as a silhouette against the sky. In fact it began life as a hunting lodge for the Hudlestones of Millom, far grander gentry than the folk just down the road, and whose chase extended way over the fells right to upper Eskdale. In terms of the Hudlestone ancestry it is a fairly recent building, because it only replaced an earlier forest lodge some time during the sixteenth century. This was Ulpha Old Hall, now no more than the stump of a fortified tower in a farmyard by the road down to Ulpha.

Today Frith Hall is a very romantic spot. The clouds are lifting as we cross the upland pastures created when the park was enclosed, where a few little dark Herdwicks are nibbling so industriously that they only have time to look up and nod briefly as we go by. On the far side of a very flimsy fence a huge bull reclines, surrounded by his harem of black-skinned beauties. Involuntarily we quicken our pace to reach the hall, where rooks are being blown cawing about the sky that is beginning to look brighter through one of the vacant windows. The ivy-covered walls are very thick, of rough stone built onto the solid rock. The fireplaces are enormous, and in the western gable is a heat-wasting external flue like the one at Coniston Hall. Probably dating from the building's later years, when it was first an inn, then a farmhouse, are a number of tiny paddocks. The Hudlestones had chosen the losing side in the civil wars of the seventeenth century, and it was the subsequent decline in their fortunes that caused the hall to become an inn. The road was used regularly by chapmen and packmen, but the situation was remote, even then, and

The Kirk at Ulpha

the place acquired a reputation for wild and unsavoury goings-on - such as the solemnisation of runaway marriages à la Gretna, robberies and murders.

The wide, windy sky is clearing now, patches of sunlight illuminating the distant fells. In the valley are the ancient farmsteads, their green fields neatly partitioned by stone walls until they dissolve into the misty cloud that softens the contours of the nearer hillsides across the river. Moving on from Frith Hall, we have to cross Blea Beck by the old bridge, where the two parapets do not match. By looking underneath, the explanation is revealed. What was originally a narrow packhorse bridge was later widened to accommodate horse-drawn traffic. Our bridlepath soon rejoins the metalled road down to Ulpha, just below the abandoned copper workings, almost completely lost in the camouflaging trees, among which, indeed, a roe deer, stepping delicately aside at our approach, loses herself effortlessly.

Now it is downhill all the way to Ulpha Bridge, past the old bobbin mill, another and less ugly reminder of the industrial inheritance of the valley. A century ago, the children from Ulpha school over the bridge would come to the mill for penny sacks of shavings to burn on the school stove. No doubt they became expert at judging exactly how long they could make the journey last without getting into trouble. At Ulpha Bridge the native rock confines the stream to a narrow confusion of white foam; upstream is a quieter tree-lined reach running under the knoll on which the church stands. Ulpha Kirk is one of the loveliest of Lakeland churches, both for its setting and for the unselfconscious dignity of its appearance.

It has been fortunate in that necessary repairs and restoration have not destroyed its traditional character. The building is really just another barn, of the same rough local stone. Inside, the beams that support the roof show the same marks of the adze. The now fragmentary wall inscriptions, some of them dated 1793, would have been quite new when Wordsworth first passed this way, neither the first nor the last pilgrim to whom the sight of this church has given a lift to the heart. Not everyone was able to reach the desired haven - the churchyard contains a memorial to James Crosbie Jenkinson of Whitehaven, who perished on Birker Moor during "the pelting of the pitiless storm" on the first of January 1926, aged seventeen.

The aspect of Dunnerdale above Ulpha begins to give credence to the wording on poor James's stone. Even the small fields of the valley floor have been wrested from a hostile environment by long, hard labour. Not even in Wasdale are the stone walls more terrifyingly impressive than those along the byway past Kiln Bank on the way up to Hoses and on, eventually, to Broughton Mills. Their cyclopean masonry will remain for the next few thousand years as the memorial to those anonymous farmers who cleared the land. The best route to take from Ulpha Bridge is, in fact, the one which brings us out near these walls; it climbs above the school, then continues through Birks Wood and on past the old Quaker burial ground. This bleak little enclosure has a sad and neglected air - not surprisingly perhaps, since no-one has been buried there for well over two hundred years. One wonders why they chose this particular spot, out in the bracken above the fell wall, because their meeting place was at Woodend, miles away over Birker Moor, not far from Devoke Water. Soon our path brings us to the vicinity of Far Kiln Bank, and the giants' walls. Following the road down, we need only cross the busier main highway below Hall Dunnerdale, to go on by Wallowbarrow Farm to the foot of the great gorge that the

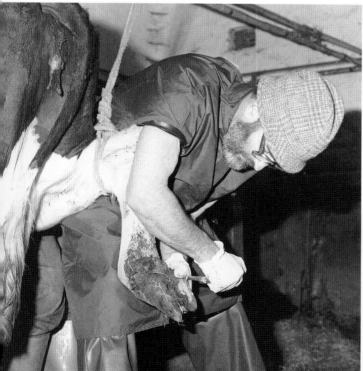

Top left;
John Hadwin, water bailiff with
spent hen salmon, Ulpha

Centre left:
Ricky Rushton (vet) treating
a cow's foot

Below:
Andrew Cain brings the library
van to the Duddon valley; Kate
Kirkwood discussing a book

Duddon has carved through the mountain. On a sunny afternoon, when the cloud has cleared, it all seems wonderfully bright, as if it belonged to another world like the music of Mozart. A word with the farmer who has brought down some of his sheep for dipping, and is penning them in his yard will soon put an end to such flights of fancy. Life in these wild valleys is hard, and can be lonely. The pitiless storms that sweep in from the Irish Sea can cut out the sun for days on end, and they bring over 100 inches of rain in an average year.

Little wonder that the track beyond the farm is squelchy, and that we have to pick our way through the wood as we approach Seathwaite. On this March afternoon, we may also encounter the wood ants. They are large, bumbling creatures, but harmless. It is said they were introduced in the hope that they would provide a change of diet for the pheasants that used to be reared hereabouts; now there are no pheasants, and the ants have multiplied. Local gardeners even use them as a seasonal marker - when the ants begin to fly, it's time to get the potatoes in!

The focal point of Seathwaite has long been the Newfield Inn, as heartwarming an objective for the traveller, in its way, as Ulpha Kirk. A quiet, peaceful scene, you might think, except perhaps when they get into the after-dinner singing at the November Shepherds' Meet. Now that there are no more quarrymen or charcoal burners, the place has to rely largely on the car-borne multitudes who pause on their way to or from the high passes at the head of the valley. They may not notice the beautifully marked slate that paves the bar, quarried from high on Walna Scar where, mercifully, the road from Coniston has never been metalled. They will certainly not be aware that it was workmen building the Seathwaite reservoir below Walna Scar who brought the Newfield an explosive moment of notoriety.

It was on July 25, 1904, a hot day, that a number of the navvies had gone down to the Travellers' Rest at Ulpha to celebrate their latest pay packet. Returning in boisterous mood late at night, they stopped at the Newfield, and demanded further refreshment. This the landlord, Thomas Dawson, refused to supply, on the ground that they had already taken on board as much as was good for them. The men accepted this with ill grace so that some went outside and, picking up whatever stones were to hand, began to smash the inn windows. Others went up the road to give church and vicarage the same treatment. The arm of the law, in the person of Sergeant Kay and his dog, well skilled at sniffing out isolated drunken navvies from the hedge bottoms where they normally fell, was not immediately to hand, so the landlord, assisted by his daughter, took the law into his own hands. They fired shots from the shattered windows with such accurate aim that one of the rioters fell dead and two others were wounded. This drastic but effective means of restoring order created such a stir that James Atkinson, Bookseller and Stationer of Ulverston, promptly brought out a pair of postcards showing the broken windows.

Dawson was later acquitted of murder, on the plea that he had been defending crown property. This was technically true, inasmuch as the Seathwaite Post Office was at that time situated in the inn, and indeed so remained until 1971 when Mr and Mrs J.Longmire retired from their long association with the Newfield. Probably this is the only post office ever to have been situated on licensed premises; and probably, too, the Newfield is the only pub ever to have served school dinners on a regular, official basis. This was during the 1940s when Seathwaite school, now closed, still had nearly fifty pupils on its roll.

Dry stone wall Kiln Bank, Duddon Valley

Seathwaite Church suffered a thorough late-nineteenth century restoration, thereby rousing John Ruskin over the hill to near apoplexy; old Parson Walker - 'Wonderful Walker', so nearly canonised by Wordsworth - would probably have had a fit, too, at the needless expense. Mrs Linton, writing in 1864, gives a commonsense antidote to the excessive sentimentality heaped on Walker by envious later generations - that he was shrewd and thrifty, a man *who knew how to turn an honest penny with the best of them, and who, by this thrift, ...managed to leave a handsome mass of savings out of an apparently beggarly income.* When Walker first brought his young bride here she was aghast, even though she had been brought up near Buttermere. She thought Seathwaite had *never before been inhabited. There were no roads, no bridges, no woods, no meadows, no neighbours.* She exaggerated, of course. More typical of the dale was one of her husband's contemporaries, commemorated in the churchyard thus:

> *Henry Turner, late of Low Moss House, undertaker of the slate quarry at Walney Scarr for 20 years, who dyed 5th July 1777, aged 49.*

For the next stage of our journey we are not strictly in the Duddon Valley at all. The rushing stream below us, on the left, is Tarn Beck, which has come down from Seathwaite Tarn - the one those unfortunate navvies were busy converting into a reservoir for Barrow-in-Furness. Above Seathwaite the fells are bigger and steeper. Viewed through a thin veil of shifting rain, the forestry plantations seem less wearyingly regimented. The sheer buttresses of rock which force the rows of trees to stop or to curve round, have helped to vary the lines and textures of the scene. So also do the pearly white waterfall ropes that tumble down between them. It is not far now to Birks Bridge. Trees continue to dominate the immediate surroundings, mainly 'yak and esh, burk and eller', as the old farmer put it. Always, there is the noise of water, and at Birks itself this can be pretty loud. A springtime diversion along the path towards Harter Fell, past more of those walls, cobbles taken as the land was cleared and piled around the resulting enclosures, rewards the walker with intoxicating scents of birch and bog myrtle, and with a view to Cockley Beck, the highest farm in the valley.

Richard Adams got to know Dunnerdale very well, when he used to stay with his family at Low Hollin Cottage below Seathwaite reservoir. He did a good deal of fell walking, and became friendly with the nearby farmers, Dennis and Gwen Williamson of Tongue. When he writes of Seathwaite and its folk, it is from direct personal experience of helping to gather sheep in the uncertain gloom of an autumn twilight, or of trying to get hay between the showers of a fickle July. But the Williamsons have a claim to distinction in their own right. Their stud of black fell ponies are as native to the hills as the Herdwick sheep. These delightful little animals were originally used for carting at the mines and quarries of the fells. Up to fourteen hands high, they are powerful and chunky in build, able to pull or carry a lot of weight. The catalogue of their virtues also includes a usually docile temperament; this, and their manageable size, make them ideal for children to ride. No doubt from the ponies' point of view this is preferable to sledding loads of slate down bumpy quarry tracks.

Yet, though the fellsides are so rough and wild, the last section of the valley bottom, between Black Hall and Cockley Beck, is remarkably flat and fertile. Jack Longmire recalled in the late 1970s how as a boy he had heard the miller at Broughton Mills claim that the Cockley Beck wheat ground into the best flour that he handled. The farm, sheltered by

Cockley Beck in winter

the traditional clump of sycamores, stands just above the highest bridge over Duddon, at the head of its own good meadowland - green, level fields, dotted in spring by the lambing ewes, Herdwicks, Swaledales and a few Jacobs. From the plantation behind the farm, the land is spread out like a counterpane across to Black Hall. The fellside is astonishingly wet, steep and stony; yet the shepherds of Dunnerdale have to climb up and down regularly, gathering their flock or looking for the odd sheep which, when found, can easily give both man and dog the slip in such a wilderness. The more distant view is inexpressibly grand, across to the Scafell crags. Then to the right, beyond the plantation, the Duddon beckons for the final stage of our present journey, along Wrynose Bottom to its birthplace in the clouds.

No person in his right mind, you would imagine, would ever try to farm here. The soil covers the land so thinly that great slabs of shining, wet rock are permanently exposed. But in Wordsworth's time Gaitscale was still occupied, up on the fellside across the river from the modern road. Parson Walker used to come up from Seathwaite to help at busy times, in the way that the dales farmers are still prepared to stand by one another. But at Gaitscale life was a struggle at best, and early in the nineteenth century, after a particularly harsh and snowy winter, less than a score of the Gaitscale flock remained alive. The people left, the sheep were joined with the Black Hall flock. No-one had the heart to resume farming in such a bleak spot, and the buildings fell rapidly into ruin.

Just outside the door of Seathwaite Church, however, a rather special stone is set into the ground. It is the stone on which Walker used to sit astride when he was helping with the clipping at Gaitscale. In an act of disinterested piety entirely characteristic of Dunnerdale, Jack Longmire and Gilbert Hartley, whose family has now farmed Turner Hall at Seathwaite for several generations, brought it down and set it up as the best possible memorial to that exemplar of a dedicated and hardworking pastor.

Hardknott Roman fort

IV: Eskdale

Stanley Ghyll or Dalegarth Force, what matters it? here is one of the choice places of the earth.

Mrs Linton.

THE FINEST way to reach Eskdale from Dunnerdale is to take the rough track which leads up Mosedale to emerge on the broad hause from which Lingcove Beck hurls itself to Throstle Garth. This is an excellent spot to have a few minutes' rest before picking our way alongside the carelessly rushing beck. From here Scafell presents an uncompromisingly craggy face, usually seamed and capped with snow until early summer. Bowfell is near enough to look really big, a properly mountain-shaped mountain, rising almost symmetrically to its graceful peak. Shelter Crags then complement Scafell - they are not so high but, along with the adjoining Crinkle Crags, more than compensate by their dark, forbidding precipices. The 'Shelter', one must assume, is on the other side, overlooking Oxendale.

But these are places for the seasoned fellwalker; we turn away to follow the leaping cascades into upper Eskdale. Sometimes the falls run white over smoothed rock into deep green pools; now the stream seems to emerge from a narrow tunnel; now there is only a fury of foam among the broken rocks. Wherever it is impossible for the wandering sheep to reach them, trees are growing, clinging to their little rootholds in the rock crevices as they overhang the water. Down at Throstle Garth the fury has abated. This is the parting of the ways, where a dainty packhorse bridge hops over the torrent. It seems like a toy, out of scale with its huge surroundings, taking the old track on to the very head of the dale below the Scafell crags. There is a little garth above the bridge not, apparently, used very much, to judge from the dilapidated condition of its walls. They are built of dark, angular stones, illuminated by bright patches of lichen. In the old days when there were more trees and the lords of the manor came up here hunting the deer, the throstles would be more in evidence than they are in our bleaker landscape: but in May-time the passer-by will be unlucky not to be rewarded by the sound of a lone cuckoo.

Now the river winds along the narrow floor of the main valley. It is still a wonderful companion. The big pools just below Throstle Garth, beneath a protecting vertical wall of bare rock, match anything that the Duddon can provide. They form a series of swimming pools, as the water glides over a natural lip of stone into the one below, until at last the stream breaks free over the pale boulders which give its middle and lower reaches such a distinctively bright and shining character. For most of the year, it is a quiet path down to Brotherilkeld at the foot of Hardknott pass. There may be a few friendly sheep about; if they are Herdwicks, they will look up as we pass to have a word with us. Some of them are dreadfully knock-kneed, but they are too well-bred to say what they think about our appearance. Looking back Bowfell, which had been hidden at Throstle Garth by the steepness of the ground, dominates the skyline again.

Ahead, the land becomes gradually less rough and stony as the valley opens out a little. There are even some stunted trees scattered over the fellside. Soon the fell walls mark the ultimate division between the open fell and the ground worth farming, however marginally. They curve round to meet at the river like pincers. In their shelter are more sheep chewing placidly, as if they had a mouthful of gum. Then through the Brotherilkeld fields, each succeeding one less stony and, in spring, greener than the last. The path now rejoins the river bank; the water runs translucent over the smooth granite stones, dappled in the sunlight by shadows of the big, old oaks that line its margin. A wooden footbridge carries another path to the farm on the opposite bank, Taw House, and then on to the higher ground, eventually to the foot of Scafell below Cam Spout.

The Romans built a fort on the relatively level land above Brotherilkeld, roughly the mid-point on their road between Ambleside and Ravenglass. For the specialist there is quite a lot to see, notably the well-preserved bath house outside the ramparts of the fort and the parade ground. But for the average visitor, the most rewarding thing is to go to the edge of the steep drop from which there is a view up towards Throstle Garth and down to the milder middle section of Eskdale and, far away, the sea. Maybe it was a certain compensation for the legionaries when they had endured days of rain and gales to look out and see the Isle of Man floating magically on a bed of soft cloud in the glow of yet another stormy sunset.

Almost immediately below Brotherilkeld is one of Eskdale's focal points - the showfield. It is best to arrive early, on the last Saturday in September, to savour the full diversity of the day. With luck the cloud will be clearing from the fells, and there will be patches of blue sky. By ten o'clock the line of pens will be filled with sheep, most of whom seem to be quite familiar with the ritual. They stand patiently, sometimes making that peculiar grinding noise with their teeth which is calculated to send tremors of anguish through the sensitive onlooker. 'Sheep' in this context, of course, (as at Wasdale) means, strictly, Herdwick sheep in all their manifestations from aged tups, via tup lambs through

Walkers, bound for Scafell Pikes, cross Lingcove Beck bridge

gimmer lambs to aged ewes, with every sort of family combination along the way - a group of one tup, any age, and four gimmers, every age; or best shearling tup and tup lamb (local). No other breeds of sheep are on show, and no other livestock. We are in the heart of the Herdwick country at these remote western daleheads.

Farther down the field the ladies are trooping in and out of the big marquee which holds the produce and handicraft sections. Along the edge of the arena the trade stands are filling up, clearly catering for the specialised clientele gathered here today; one announces Someone's Sheep-dip, in bold letters; Someone Else is 'Way Ahead in Worming'. One farmer has been helping his wife to unload the Land Rover, and outside the marquee is a line of majestic carrots flanked by enormous 'mangold-wurtzells' and swedes. There is nothing dainty about the produce classes.

Not far away are tall racks, forming three sides of a small square. Here are one or two older men already, in their best clothes: flat caps, rather tightly fitting tweed jackets, shiny boots turned up a little at the toes. They are pulling sticks and crooks out of the canvas bags they have brought, and slotting them carefully into the racks. As they do so, they cast po-faced glances at the other entries. Soon there are dozens of them, mostly highly polished, with elegantly shaped horn handles. A separate section caters for the ornamental sticks that have been embellished with naturalistic carvings - usually linked with the local scene, a terrier, a fox's head, a woodpecker or a pheasant. As with the other sections, from sheep to swedes, the non-exhibitor can simply enjoy the variety and artistry of it all.

There is no end to the range of this show. They have roped off a ring where presently the dogs will be paraded for judging - strictly functional again: shepherds' dogs, foxhounds and terriers. By early afternoon, when this is going on, the cloud has cleared, so that the sunshine is lighting up the golds and browns of the bracken on the slopes above, as well as the huntsman's red coat as he leads two chosen hounds into the ring. They look benevolent enough here, tails gently waving like inverted pendulums, ribs clearly marked through their shining coats. The little terriers have much less sense of occasion, and are liable to spoil their chance of an award by pulling at the lead, or leaping ferociously at some other competitor. One man has apparently just brought his dog for the sake of his company; we have already seen him several times, wandering vaguely round with the lead in one hand and a half-empty tankard in the other. The beer tent, it should be explained, is by some margin the largest on the field.

During the afternoon all the family and friends have arrived, the tension of the judging is over, and everyone can relax. There are the children's sports, the fell races, the hound trails to beguile the time between gossiping with folk perhaps not seen since last year's show. Most of the dale children have come, and they hurl themselves along the roughly marked track with tremendous zest, especially the tiny ones, precariously clutching their time-honoured eggs and spoons. The climax of their sports is the fell race, up a fairly gentle oblique path above the field which would lead over to Dunnerdale if a person went far enough. And then the climax of the entire afternoon arrives with the men's fell race. No longer is the path acceptable: the young men have to toil right to the stony skyline of the fell, whence they pour back in giant leaps, for all the world like the fearsome invaders who first gave their names to Brotherilkeld or Taw. No wonder perhaps, that the terriers, still being guided round the ring, feel a bit excited.

The hound trails punctuate the afternoon with another kind of excitement which,

Scafells from Border End

except for the owners, owes most to the odds chalked on the bookies' blackboards. The start is tense and noisy - a line of straining hounds waiting to be slipped at starter's orders. The sheep in the opposite field gather in a bunch to see what is going on; as the dogs fly past, devouring the far wall in their rush, they all turn their heads to watch then slowly scatter over the field again. Now the spectators must find something to engage their attention until the finish, which is even noisier than the start. The owners are waiting at the line, and as soon as the leading hound is spotted in the distance, everyone begins to shout or whistle or wave a brightly colour scarf. Maybe the finish will be close, and then we will all get excited too, as the hounds streak over the last level field to the basin of food that they know awaits them.

Little remains by this time except the final jollifications. The boys are still slugging each other with pillows as they try to keep their balance astride a greasy pole. The man with the tankard has stopped to offer his dog a swig from its golden depths. The sheep, almost forgotten, are stamping the ground in their cramped pens, with resignation or because they are getting very hungry. From the driver's window of a Land Rover parked by the ringside, a well-booted leg is sticking out, and its owner is prone across the length of the front seats. Ladies are taking their cushions, pieces of patchwork, marmalade or rum butter from the produce tent, and no doubt will presently roust their menfolk out of the still packed beer tent; from outside the noise of the conversations within sounds rather like a flock of starlings come to roost in a tree. There will be no danger, at any rate, of them getting drunk on their prize money. One hopes the luckier winners, too, are carefully looking after their supplementary awards given by the various firms represented on the trade stands - a footrot knife, a bag of rough ewe and lamb food or a body warmer.

For those with the stamina to stay, the show is rounded off by more specialised contests like hornblowing and singing, but we still have the body of Eskdale before us, calling out for exploration. It is not far along the road to Boot, but the motorist sees little beyond the ribbon of tarmac ahead and the stone walls on each side. Far better to return to the foot of Hardknott and walk by the footpath behind Wha House, to reach this tiny village in the heart of the dale. At the height of summer it almost vanishes beneath the tide of visitors, but on a mild and misty December morning it is calm and peaceful. The tones of grey give a delicate pastel effect to the landscape; soft folds of cloud cling to the dripping fellsides. The oldest houses, built, like the massive field walls, of irregular blocks of local granite, look as if they have grown out of the earth. Standing on the narrow stone bridge that crosses Willan Beck, we can see that a race has been constructed from a point above the roaring falls to the two water-wheels on the side of the nearby mill.

The Lake District Special Planning Board has restored the mill to working order, so that it is possible to see one of the wheels in action. It works on the overshot principle: water clatters into the buckets from the wooden launder, and the wheel whizzes round, more water splashing off in a shower of spray. Inside is a drying kiln - oats, the usual grain crop when the dales had to be largely self-supporting for food, need a good deal of drying, especially at the end of a typically wet Lakeland summer. Above the peat fire is a slate lattice covered by perforated metal squares where the grain is spread out. When it is dry, it is shovelled through a hole in the wall into a hopper inside the mill itself. The hopper feeds the grindstones and the meal descends through a chute to the mill floor. Old records show that this has been the site of Eskdale Mill since at least the thirteenth century. The second

Right:
Arthur Irvine,
stick maker,
Eskdale

Left:
Eskdale showfield,
Brotherilkeld

wheel dates from an enlargement of the premises as recently as 1842.

Walking back through the village, and crossing the quiet fields beyond the main road, we soon reach St. Catherine's Church, probably even older than the mill, though the building we see now is the product of a very thorough restoration - ie. rebuilding in 1881. In the churchyard there is a striking monument to a local personality who was at the height of his career when that restoration took place. Tommy Dobson was master of the Eskdale and Ennerdale foxhound pack for fifty-three years until his death at the age of eighty-three in 1910. The granite stone is carved to show Tommy's face in high relief; the suggestion of a smile plays about the firm mouth. Then the sculptor added the heads of fox and hound, and completed his composition with two hunting horns, one straight, the other curved.

Not far upstream from the churchyard, the course of an old railway runs above the river, which once it crossed by an iron bridge to serve a mine on the farther bank. It is easy to trace this line back to Boot. In winter the only activity is likely to be that of the crows excavating for grubs in the fields. Birch trees grow through the mossy, lichened wall which once separated the line from the adjoining pastures. Not surprisingly, the railroad brings us directly to the deserted platform of Dalegarth station, terminus of the Ravenglass and Eskdale Railway. Originally, of course, there was nothing of the paraphernalia of a railway station here. A short distance up the line (ie. down the valley) the track passes right in front of what was once a row of miners' cottages. Above the cottages are more abandoned iron workings. Between these and the mill is a line of low, ruinous buildings. They are on the loading wharf to which a railway siding ran. At one end is the ore store; a tramway runs up from the wharf to the spoil heaps that mark the adit to the mine.

Eskdale's industrial past represents only a brief chapter in its long history. The iron mines, for the benefit of which the railway was constructed in 1875, were worked for only a few years after that date. The granite quarries, however, continued to ship their stone down the valley. Then in 1915 'La'al Ratty' took on its present appearance when the track was altered to narrow gauge. It would be tempting in the holiday season, to leave Eskdale by rail, and go along the 'back' of Muncaster fell to Ravenglass.

A whistle from somewhere near the miners' cottages creates a murmur of expectation on the platform. A score of cameras is poised, a straggle of dads and little boys gather at the turn-table. The tiny engine, spick and span, everything polishable polished to the last degree of brilliance, puffs gently in. The open seats are the best, even though there may be a slight risk of getting a piece of grit in your eye. Some of the dads have put the rest of the family aboard and rushed off in the car, sometimes to the hazard of other road users, to get another photograph from the bridge at Eskdale Green. Dad has the worst of the bargain, driving down to Ravenglass. We can sit back, watching the sheep gallop away at our approach, and savouring the farm smells. We halt at a passing loop to allow a special train to come by, engine straining under the weight of a full load of railway buffs. Then on we go again, winding so much that at times a passenger at the back of the train can see the engine almost passant, to use the heraldic term, until we meander past Muncaster Mill and look over the tidal flats of the triple estuary.

The drawback about going to Ravenglass by the railway is that you don't see half of Eskdale. On your next visit, therefore, walk resolutely away from Boot, and take the byway opposite what used to be the village school. This is the road to one of the most striking bits of scenery in the Lake District - Stanley Gill. The metalled road runs only as far as

'La'al Ratty'. Train leaving Dalegarth bound for Ravenglass

Dalegarth Hall, and then the way becomes a path which diminishes in size as it increases in difficulty. At first the track is through woodland where, in early summer, we are soon made aware of the presence of exotic rhododendrons shining amid the more normal Lakeland tree cover. Well away from traffic now, the smell of petrol has been replaced by whiffs of conifer. The stream below is very inadequately confined by its banks, and splashes ever nearer to the path as we enter the gorge. Climbing steadily, we now come to a wooden bridge high above the water. What with the rhododendrons, the thick moss, the tall trees growing out of the precipitous rock face and the water dripping everywhere, it is rather like one's romantic image of Nepal. The gorge has grown so narrow that it can be spanned by a fallen tree: the sky is no more than a slice of grey-blue light, filtered through the foliage so that the rock face, stained every imaginable shade of green, shines with an unnatural brightness. The path continues as far as the splendid waterfall by which the stream enters the gorge from the open moor, breaking as it falls into ever-changing lines of fine spray.

Having retraced our steps to Dalegarth Hall, we may take the old bridleway down to Forge Bridge near the King George IV Inn. This seems a quiet walk through peaceful woods: but here and there we notice how the winter storms have brought down one of the big, old conifers, earth and stones attached to the disc that was its root system, and a smooth surface of solid bedrock revealed where the roots had probed uselessly for a more secure hold. The only sounds are the thin cheeps and trills that tell of unseen tiny birds in the treetops. Beyond the wood, the bridleway approaches more closely the river; fragments of a cobbled surface as it climbs over a natural rock outcrop bear witness to its greater importance in the pre-motor age as a way into the heart of the dale. From a bluff overlooking the sparkling stream we can look back and see Bowfell still, now a distant peak, watching over its valley.

The next working farm after Dalegarth is Milkingstead, but before then we pass a ruined settlement. Only a Wordsworth could do justice to the gentle sadness of its atmosphere. Two ancient gooseberry bushes are flourishing at the back; the road runs straight through the carefully cobbled yard where the byres and stable, huge undressed blocks of granite encrusted with moss and lichens, are plainly decipherable. As we leave, on tiptoe for fear of disturbing the spirits of the place, a harsh pheasant croaks from the nearby plantation, and we meet the first people we have seen since Dalegarth. A delightful little suspension bridge at Milkingstead points across to the main road, but we continue over the fields to Forge Bridge. A group of store cattle is foraging among the trees which run down to the edge of the pasture; all except one, who is systematically scratching his back on a conveniently horizontal branch.

Forge Bridge is another reminder of the industrial associations of Eskdale, but the village of Eskdale Green, just up the road, reflects a quite different strand in the make-up of the dale. In its present form, straggling along the highway, it is a product of speculative building at the end of the nineteenth century, when some of the local landowners saw an opportunity to cash in on the expanding tourist industry. However, the lighter colour of the stone gives the houses a slightly more cheerful aspect than those inflicted on Coniston, for example, at the same period. The drier and sunnier climate out here also enables the householders to create wonderfully bright little gardens, some of which spill right out over their retaining walls.

Returning to Forge Bridge and beyond, the way down Eskdale proper takes off to the right, opposite the hunt kennels. This lowest stretch of the valley consists almost entirely of mossland and pasture. The flat fields are dotted with molehills; the hedge bottoms in springtime crowded with celandines and primroses. The farms are situated in a line above flood level, and their names are a litany of the archetypal Lake District as the road twists and heaves past their road-ends - Knott End, Cragg, Howbank, Ellerbeck. This last-named farm is almost on the A595, by which it takes only a few minutes to drive to Holmrook, en route for Wasdale.

First, however, turn left, and then follow the byroad towards the estuary, to Hall Waberthwaite. The name, according to Ekwall, means 'the hunting or fishing shed situated in a forest clearing', and to stand at the corner of St. John's churchyard, looking over the tidal flats, is to feel that little has changed since the first Scandinavian settlers arrived and created that clearing. Immediately beneath the churchyard wall the Esk winds to the saltings, blue in summer with sea lavender, then to the wider, bird-haunted spaces bounded by the sand dunes where Esk, Irt and Mite converge. Once there was a ford here and the vicar, who was also responsible for the church over the way at Muncaster, used to alter service times in accordance with the tides. In the churchyard are the remains of two pre-Norman preaching crosses. (There is another at Muncaster.) The church interior is relatively modern. The carved oak pulpit is dated 1630, and bears a Latin inscription for the edification of the preacher: *Woe is me if I preach not the Truth.* The box pews have survived intact since 1807.

This unpretentious little building in the forest clearing is a witness to the continuity of life in the valley, and makes a perfect counterpoint to the desolate grandeur surrounding the ancient garth above Brotherilkeld; and both together bring vividly to mind Thomas Hardy's thoughts on real permanence amid the rise and fall of dynasties. "Ah," said an old farmer at Boot when I asked him whereabouts in the valley he lived: "I live in paradise."

I WILL LIFT UP MINE EYES
UNTO THE HILLS
FROM WHENCE
COMETH MY
STRENGTH.

Church window detail,
Wasdale Head

V: Wasdale

You have entered within the gates of one of Nature's grandest temples, and have caught the echo of some of her noblest harmonies.

Mrs Linton.

RAVENGLASS is a busy spot during the holiday season. It is the starting point for the miniature railway through Miterdale into Eskdale; close by are the superb rhododendron gardens of Muncaster Castle; immediately to boot, as it were, are numbers of first-class low-level walks. But don't overlook the old main street, where you will be repulsed by its abrupt termination if the tide is high, for the sea comes right up to the fortress-like houses that back directly onto the estuary. The Irt, northernmost of the three rivers that wind across the muddy sand at low tide, is the one which has come down from Wasdale. At Holmrook, a few miles father along the A595, we can turn right for Irton, where the journey to the head of the dale may most conveniently begin.

Not that Irton is a clearly defined village; more a scatter of farms. If it were not for the signpost to the church, a casual visitor would not know he was in, or near, Irton; even that such a place existed. But the rewards for turning off along the unmade track, carried on a broad dyke above the surrounding fields, are great. The church is in the middle of acres of well-kept farmland; its churchyard surely has the finest long-distance view of any in the kingdom, because from here we can see the mountain group at the head of Wasdale. As Bowfell stands above Eskdale, so Great Gable dominates the Wasdale scene, and most theatrically. It is not just the striking shape of the mountain that draws the eye; the morning

56

sunlight shows up with piercing clarity those fearful sawn-off crags below the summit. Under the dark rolling lines of cloud which threaten to come down and cut out that sunlight, it is not a friendly prospect.

But the reason for coming to the church was not only to get a preliminary glimpse of our destination. There is much of interest close at hand. In the churchyard is Irton cross, ten feet high and carved over a thousand years ago from a single block of red sandstone. Scholars believe that it was set up early in the ninth century before the arrival of the Scandinavian settlers who made a cross of their own at Gosforth, a few miles to the north. Most of the carving which covers all four faces of the shaft has withstood the Cumbrian weather so well that the patterning is still plain to see. On the two narrow sides vine scrolls swirl and spiral upwards (vines, indeed: what did dwellers in west Cumberland know about vines?) The two broad faces are divided into panels carved with delicately interlacing lines and rosettes with fret and step patterning. The whole impression given by the cross suggests that it may be linked with the flowering of Christian civilisation in Ireland, to which we also owe the inspiration for many of the similar early crosses which have survived in western Scotland and the Isles.

Having looked up at Gable, and examined the cross, it would be easy to dismiss the church itself, heavy-looking and cement-rendered, and press on with eager feet to Santon Bridge. This would be a mistake, because the church interior shows that not all Victorian rebuildings were academic and uninspired. This one has a bright, cheerful and friendly atmosphere, owing not a little to the extraordinary windows. These alone are worth a journey to see, because they illustrate the scriptures instead of simply commemorating a benefactor by the representation of a pallid, characterless angel or saint. Noah peers out of the ark, newly stranded on Mount Ararat, no doubt wondering where he is. In one of the chancel windows a party of very glum looking Israelites are gathering manna, much resembling mushrooms, in the wilderness. Since the dedication is to Saint Paul, he figures largely too: a streak of lightning on the road to Damascus; pleading his cause before King Agrippa; participating in a realistic Maltese shipwreck. Then, on the north wall, is a series of four windows designed by Burne-Jones, and manufactured by William Morris & Co. It forms a wonderful climax to the riches of this stained glass.

Yet still we cannot go - why are there six elaborately embroidered banners hanging in the nave? If a member of the congregation felt he had exhausted the resources of the windows during a dull sermon he could turn to these because, here again, in the mediaeval tradition, is material for instruction or meditation. One portrays Christ carrying a lamb; another bears the symbols of the four Evangelists; a third, most unusually, is a representation of the Trinity. The remaining banners illustrate the Cross, the Lamb of God and symbols associated with Saint Paul. In the late 1980s the tiny but devoted congregation of this astonishing church had these banners cleaned and professionally restored, so that now they make the same impact on the worshipper as when they were installed in 1871, and correctly described in the *Whitehaven News* of the day as *exquisite specimens of art*.

From Irton to Santon Bridge much of the landscape is pleasantly park-like, no doubt due to the presence of Irton Hall, once a 'gentleman's seat'. Santon Bridge is exactly what the name implies, a handsome single span, close by the inn of the same name. The narrow way deeper into Wasdale is on the right just before the bridge, its steep banks starred with primroses in springtime, but the scene of many a traffic jam in summer. Soon the road begins to climb and then, at a sharp right-hand bend, the mountains which were hidden from the neighbourhood of Santon Bridge come into view once more. The land hereabouts is very rough pasture where it has not been planted with larch or spruce. We could continue directly to Wastwater foot by Wasdale Hall but, in order to get the full flavour of Wasdale, it is better to diverge from this road to the delightful little settlement known variously as Strands or Nether Wasdale.

The houses and inns are brightly painted, the stonework round the windows picked out in some strongly contrasting colour, in the old Cumberland tradition. There is no order about the place; every building is unique, each one set at a different angle to the road, with no regularity of spacing between them. On the little green separating the Screes Hotel and Strands Hotel is a remarkable monument to that outbreak of generosity among the local gentry in the 1880s which contributed so richly to Irton church. This, however, is a purely secular structure, presented to the village in 1880 by Mrs Eleanor Irton of Calder Abbey. It is a large stone-built drinking fountain, now mellowed by honeysuckle growing on its roof. All creatures great and small are provided for: a trough for the horses on one side; a stone seat on the other; in front, a basin at dog-lapping height; inside, a tap for humans, placed above a stone slab with a neat hole in the centre, so that it looks like an old-fashioned lavatory seat for dwarves. Alas, the tap no longer works, and the iron cup which must have been attached by a chain to the stout ring in the side wall has vanished.

Another relic of those more leisured days stands on the green outside the neat little rectangular church - a maypole, erected to celebrate Queen Victoria's Diamond Jubilee. This is at the bottom end of the village. Walk up to the top end, a pleasant stroll. There is no hustle or bustle; but each of the hotels is having its windows cleaned, quietly and methodically, and a man with rake and grass-hook, straight out of *The Pilgrim's Progress*, is clearing brambles from the roadside. At the top of the hill stands the Low Wood Hall Hotel, yet another reminder of Strands' high Victorian noon. In its gardens, running down to the village below, two magnificent stone lions, one at each end of the roof, guard the vast high glasshouses.

Wordsworth said that this is the route by which a visitor must enter Wasdale, so here we are dutifully preparing ourselves for the experience. *The principal entrance is from the open country by Strands*, he wrote in 1810. *This...is much the best approach. Wastdale is well worth the notice of the traveller who is not afraid of fatigue; no part of the country is more distinguished by sublimity.* He was right, of course. The cosy domesticity of Strands and the varied woods do not prepare us for the shock when the road emerges from their shelter and descends to within a few feet of the margin of the lake. The great Baddeley permitted himself a purple passage at this point: *...the middle and far distance is the quintessence of wildness... There is a unity of spirit in the whole, and a beauty and grandeur of outline in the surrounding fells seldom if ever found in combination elsewhere in Britain.* Mrs Linton and her husband unwisely came into Wasdale over Styhead in their tour of 1864, and they didn't recover their equanimity until they reached Strands, with an audible sigh of relief: a garden, and a shrubbery are *evidence of home and human care...we cannot make a home on the wilds, or pitch our tent on the hill-tops.*

Yet, for centuries, a few unconquerable spirits have made their home in those wilds. Apart from the parked vehicles, the scene looking down on Wasdale Head is still as Wordsworth knew it: *...a little chapel and half a dozen neat dwellings scattered upon a plain*

Overbeck and silver birch

of meadow and corn ground intersected with stone walls apparently innumerable, like a large piece of lawless patchwork... Beyond this little fertile plain lies, within a bed of steep mountains, the long, narrow, stern and desolate lake of Wastdale. Somehow, they manage to find space within this fertile plain, to hold a shepherds' meet on the second Saturday of every October. No-one but the shepherds and their Herdwicks could have survived here for so long, and made a living into the bargain.

Back near Wasdale Hall, in convoy with two Land Rovers each pulling a trailer full of sheep, we see the morning sun pick out the restless agitated skyline above the Screes. Wastwater is as dark as the broken rock that tumbles to its shore. Cloud is trailing on the summits of Gable and Scafell, giving promise of a fine day after overnight rain. It is wet underfoot when we get out of the car, and a fresh wind blows chill over the field where the lines of pens are set out, each boldly labelled with an exhibitor's name.

Hours of preparation have already gone into making the sheep ready to be shown. Ten days ago they were washed and given a dressing of red ruddle, then washed again. This ruddle, which they once dug from the top of the Screes, but prosaically now buy from the Farmers' Supply Company, is really a cosmetic, the better to show off the carefully brushed coats. By show day all the loose red dust will have come off. The rams will have had their horns washed and polished so that they shine; the ewes, hornless, get away with just having their faces washed. There they stand, in their little enclosure, waiting for the judging to begin, and very fine they look. A good Herdwick holds its head high, has a prominent eye, and the white ears are quite sharp. The aged rams have a wonderfully patriarchal appearance, their great curling horns springing from the back of their massive heads.

At ten o'clock prompt about fifteen farmers take out of their pens one of these majestic fellows for the first judging class. The winner will gain applause from his peers and one litre of Oramec. They line up along the central gangway, each holding his charge by the horns, nervously giving his wool a last smoothing by hand. One restless fellow rears onto his hind legs; another lugs his owner temporarily clean out of line. The judge looks built to cope with any emergency, however. Quite young, the size of a rugby forward, hatless and with an open-necked shirt, even in this wind, pale blue long-sleeved jersey, waterproof overtrousers and enormous clogs, he moves silently along the line, first standing back to look, then running his hand over the coats. A good animal will have clean white legs - no black once the shearling stage is past - and be short from knee to fetlock, with a good sound foot. The coat should show white bristle at the nape of the neck, shine like silver just behind the front legs, and be grey-blue underneath when you open out the wool along the side. The judge may also feel the shoulder to see whether it is good. Then, to move things on a stage further, he gestures to the exhibitors to let the rams go. He watches intently as they walk back and forward in the enclosure, mainly to check how they move. A ram might be bad on either back or front legs, a defect which would not show while he was being held. Another gesture, and all the exhibitors dive onto their own exhibits (an innocent visitor might wonder how they recognise which one is theirs), thereby re-establishing the original line. Now the judge moves silently along once more, feeling a shoulder here, and examining teeth there - they may be slack, and he should not be able to feel an edge on them (if he can, they are not well set for grazing).

At last he is ready to shuffle the pack. A tall young fellow is consigned to the far end of the line. It's a bit like the Last Judgement, even to the gnashing of teeth. One nervous

Sheep graze on the shore of Wastwater; The Screes form a dramatic backdrop

exhibitor is tickling his charge's neck. The top end of the line is now being shuffled again, by silent moves of the judge's hand. He stands back to survey the line impassively, checks the feel of a shoulder yet again, stands back once more. Then, by raising an eyebrow, he summons the steward who rushes forward with the gaudy winners' rosettes - often running as far as the top six exhibits in a class.

The judge needs to be economical of word and gesture, partly because he will know all the exhibitors, and there must be no suggestion that he is unduly friendly towards anyone; but also because he will be on his feet in that enclosure for most of the next six hours. There are twenty-nine classes, some of them remarkably complicated - best aged ram, shearling ram and ram lamb. How do you balance groups of three against each other? The judge has to weigh in his mind that the old fellow in this group isn't very good in the tooth, but the shearling in that group is a bit spindly in the leg, yet yon third group, with indifferent oldsters, includes a ram lamb that has the makings of a future champion... Even among the western dales, Wasdale Shepherds' Meet is the supreme Herdwick festival.

Other things do go on, certainly. These days, a shepherds' meet is a show in all but name. There is no need to foregather, as they did when Canon Rawnsley accompanied a friend to a spot near the summit of Helvellyn to exchange strays: then, between 100 and 150 were regularly returned to their native heafs every July. Now, if there is a stranger or two when you bring the sheep down for clipping or dipping, you identify their owner's marks, pick up the telephone, and your neighbour from the far side of the mountain comes round with his trailer. So the social aspect of the meets has assumed a greater importance.

Alongside the judging enclosure it is all rather serious, not to say solemn. The spectators converse in undertones, as if they were in a cathedral. An elderly man with a crook, who might be mistaken for an Old Testament prophet, gives a quiet word of advice to a young exhibitor. Even attempts at jocularity fall flat. One devoted farmer's wife is holding a sheep's head firm while her husband applies a final wet cloth to its face. Meanwhile the man at the adjoining pen startles them by giving one of his group a resounding thwack with the flat of his hand. A cloud of red dust fills the air; "Just a last-minute job this morning," he says, but no-one smiles. Not that the atmosphere at Wasdale Head is conducive to levity, even when the sun shines. It is a dour place; the piped music from the public address system does nothing to promote cheerfulness, in spite of its best endeavour, by relaying songs from the 1940s - "Here we are again, happy as can be," or sanitised country-style arrangements of alleged hunting songs: nobody who valued his life would cry "Tally-ho" in Wasdale. The arrival of the Black Combe beagles is only a momentary diversion. The excitable little hounds mill round the ring for five minutes, tails wagging, scrabbling for the morsels the huntsman has thrown to them. They are rather like a party of young schoolboys on an outing. Then the huntsman sounds a baleful note on his horn, and they are all spirited away.

It may have been because the sun had come out, but with the advent of the hound trails, everyone cheered up at last. Wasdale Head is perhaps the ideal venue for this sport, because the trail can be laid over the higher ground round the dalehead, so that the hounds are visible for practically the whole circuit. They provided a continued diversion as we walked from the showfield past Burnthwaite Farm to the foot of the Sty Head Pass. Even when we couldn't see a trail we could hear it, and the sight and sound of the dogs racing along the fellside is strangely exhilarating. In an attempt to find a good station for David's

Wastwater. In the background Scafell Pike (3,206 feet) and Scafell (3,162 feet)

photography, we became almost too closely involved. At one point the trail swooped down through an open gate, across the bridleway, over the stream at its side, then over the field wall beyond - a sort of Becher's jump in reverse. This was very exciting, because many of the hounds failed to clear the wall, dropped back into the stream, and had to scramble back over the wall as best they could. Exciting for us as spectators, but not dignified for the competitors, who soon had their revenge. A few yards down the path, the next trail would shortly be crossing in the opposite direction. The opportunity was too good to be missed. David crouched below the wall at the edge of the stream, ready to photograph the flying hounds. On they came, but checked at the wall. Only one crossed at the point of camera focus where the aniseed rag had passed. The rest recoiled to jump better, and came swirling over the wall straight onto, and around, him before picking up the scent anew.

Burnthwaite Farm provides a foundation for Wordsworth's positive comments about Wasdale Head. In the midst of its quiet fields, sheltered by its surrounding trees, the whole place luxuriated in the late afternoon sun. Mr and Mrs Linton need not have gone to Strands for that glimpse of human care and domesticity. A black and white duck, ducklings in tow, was foraging for scraps in the grassy paddock behind the farm; a flock of comfortable-looking hens was sunbathing below the rhododendrons along the garden wall; a pet lamb was nibbling the grass. Nobody was about - probably everyone was at the shepherds' meet. No sound could be heard but the whispering of the stream as we walked back to the church, Wastwater a distant silver gleam.

This church, like Saint Paul's at Irton, is situated by itself in the fields, only these are hard-won fields, walled with thick dykes of stone, and sometimes having massive piles of stone also cleared from the land to make cultivation possible within their bounds. It is truly the church for the dale, as it always has been. A note in the 'guide' reminds us that the churchwardens' staves have a Herdwick ram's head carved on the one, and a ewe's on the other. They were made in 1982 by a local stickmaker. But most of the visitors who file into the church do so on account of its associations with the climbers who are buried in the chapel garth, or to find the diamond-shaped pane of glass engraved as their common aspiration and memorial.

Climbing the high fells for the sake of doing so, much less their sheer rock bastions, was not a thing that the people who lived here ever thought of doing, except in special circumstances. If you were gathering sheep, or hunting the foxes that preyed upon them, that was one thing; but to go up there in cold blood, as it were, was another matter altogether. Wordsworth's poem *The Brothers*, written in the 1790s, indicates how the shepherds habitually ranged over the highest tops. At about the same date Joseph Budworth hired a guide and took a flask of brandy to help him scale Coniston Old Man; and gradually more and more adventurous visitors broadened the scope of their explorations. The heroic age of Lakeland rock climbing, as distinct from fell walking, came later, and was based on Wasdale.

Most of the pioneers were university men, officially in the Lake District as members of 'reading parties' - W.P.Haskett-Smith who first climbed Napes Needle on Great Gable solo in 1886, then repeated the feat as a jubilee celebration fifty years later, was from Eton and Trinity, Oxford. R.Pendlebury, who is commemorated by the Pendlebury Traverse, a variation on the ordinary route on the east face of Pillar Rock, was from Saint John's, Cambridge. Batting for the locals, however, was J.W.Robinson of Whinfell Hall,

Black Combe beagles at Wasdale Show

Cockermouth. He could match even the legendary Haskett-Smith feat for feat, and often accompanied him on perilous ascents. Then there were the Abraham brothers from Keswick, George and Ashley, who not infrequently added cumbersome photographic equipment to their burden of ropes.

They took what would now be regarded as quite unacceptable risks in their bare-knuckle contests with the mountain crags. In O.G.Jones' *Rock Climbing in the English Lake District*, the author describes an incident in a difficult ascent with the Abraham brothers. The three of them were climbing Scafell Pinnacle from Deep Ghyll: *We cleared away the loose stones from our platform. It shelved badly downwards and offered no guarantee of safety in case I fell from the next vertical bit. But George sturdily rammed his brother close against the wall, and intimated that the two of them would accept the responsibility of fielding me if necessary. I mounted their shoulders, and reached up at arm's length to a sharp and firm edge of rock. A preliminary grind of my boot into a shoulder blade, and then a clear swing out on the arms, a desperate pull-up with knees and toes vainly seeking support, and at last the upper shelf was mounted. But we were all breathless.* A classic Jones under-statement, one feels.

Haskett-Smith, writing in the *Fell and Rock Journal* in 1921, recalled some of the more endearingly eccentric characters of forty years previously: Charles Packe, who delighted in passing nights on the loftiest and bleakest spots which he could find. His own weird contrivance for this purpose, the original mountain tent in a way, was not unlike a huge spectacle case, or a canvas canoe. By the 1880s this was so ancient and hard that he was not much better off than a mediaeval knight trying to sleep in plate armour. F.H.Bowring, another Trinity man, was always organising everybody. He made up his mind on one occasion that two youths who had not returned to Wasdale Head had fallen off Pikes Crag. (In fact, they had merely walked over Sty Head, and were reposing comfortably at Rosthwaite.) He led the company forth from the Huntsman's Inn, as the Wastwater Hotel was then known, in cataracts of rain. Dusk was closing in as he urged them to examine Pikes Crag for the third time, adding testily: "But this rain is very unfortunate. I'm afraid we shall not find anything of interest."

The hotel was well named, for the landlord, Will Ritson, was passionately fond of hunting. He also contrived to establish for himself the reputation of a larger-than-life character, which has now lasted for a century and more. Haskett-Smith, from his lofty Oxonian height, observed that many of the retorts on which he especially prided himself were, like some of the great Dr Johnson's, rather ponderously rude. Miss E.C.Douglas, contributing to the *Fell and Rock Journal* in 1913, recalled that *we* (ie. the ladies) *did not care much for him; he was rough in manner, and not attractive to children, and was always prophesying danger, and had no sympathy with our desire to climb. His wife was a dear, and whenever she saw us in Mosedale, she brought us delicious milk, and cake of her own baking.*

Happy days. A person would need gallons of milk today to succour all the ladies in the climbing parties trudging past the hotel. At the height of the holiday season, you feel that something akin to the destination boards that they have at railway stations would not come amiss. Wasdale Head: for Yewbarrow, Mosedale to Steeple and Pillar, Kirk Fell, Great Gable, Great End, Scafell and Lingmell. What a destination board! What a stirring roll call for the fell walker as well as the rock climber! Our track is the one over the packhorse bridge, where Mrs Ritson came with refreshments for the young ladies, up to Black Sail Pass for Ennerdale.

Gurning at Egremont Crab Fair

VI: Ennerdale

Until Ennerdale has the benefit of carriageways along its banks, it will remain comparatively a terra incognita to the tourist world, save those who can brave a rough pass, and those who care only to gape away an hour at the foot whilst their horses are baiting at the inn...for ever after quite contented with the belief that they have seen Ennerdale, and 'done' the lake effectively.

Mrs Linton.

THE SHORTEST route from Wasdale to Ennerdale is strictly for able-bodied pedestrians - over the Black Sail Pass between Kirkfell and Looking Stead. Once embarked on the easy part of the walk, downhill and past Black Sail Hut, we can see how different this valley is from any other in the Lake District. In its upper reaches it is a deep green trough, cut through steep, high mountains, almost claustrophobic in their dominating presence. The reason for the greenness is the much abused forestry planting, which runs right down to Ennerdale Water. Perhaps those who carp would have preferred to approach the valley with Baddeley, a century and more ago, from the track by Floutern Tarn. There was no forest in those days; but, looking seawards: *a veritable 'black country' (except that it is red with iron ore) extends over the comparative flats to the sea, and the prospect is further disfigured by a huge chimney close to the outlet of Ennerdale Lake.* To each period, the distraction of its own particular economic preoccupation. In 1990 the only haematite mine to remain open is the Florence and Ullcoats near Egremont, and even here plans are being made to allow visitors access to the workings as an off-beat tourist attraction.

In fact, much of the Ennerdale planting is now mature and, as in all the big Lake District forests, a carefully considered policy of felling and replanting is in operation. The head forester looks years ahead in his planning, perhaps arranging for some anticipatory felling so that regeneration has begun before a larger area nearby is clear-felled.

Forestry is one of the largest industries in the Lake District; highly skilled workmen operate enormous machines that harvest the fifty-year-old trees, amounting to over 50,000 tonnes annually from the whole region. The manner in which the Forestry Commission is following up the extraction of timber from Ennerdale becomes apparent as we walk along the track, now below Black Sail Hut a forestry road. Land that has been clear-felled inevitably looks like a disaster area for a comparatively short time; in Ennerdale some of these sections have been wholly or partially replanted mainly with conifers; other have been altered in shape, or replanted with broad-leaved trees, or simply left clear. The preferred option from these possible choices has been determined by the surrounding land form. In consultation with landscape architects, the commission is taking pains to ensure that in the future Ennerdale Forest will positively enhance the appearance of the valley.

Blanket monoculture planting is definitely no longer an option. The opportunity is taken, when replanting, to increase the diversity of the forest - spruce, larch, Douglas fir, pines, broadleaves, all have a part to play. There will be a greater range of species on the lower slopes and in the valley bottom: open spaces of different shapes and sizes will be created, particularly along the River Liza, so that in time the overall effect will be pleasantly varied and more 'natural' looking. This objective is being achieved by the application of design principles to the landscape. The forester considers the scale and shape of his plantation in relation to the nearby crags and the angle of the slopes. The precise mix of trees to achieve a degree of diversity and visual delight will depend on the land use pattern, and the need to create an overall unity of effect right through the valley. There has to be a subtle balancing act to obtain the right proportions between forest cover and the bare rocky slopes of the mountains. Thus, towards the higher ground, it is better to fell or plant bigger areas, where distant perspectives will allow the bold land forms to dominate, and vegetation patterns are simpler; but in the valley bottom, where the scale is more intimate, and land use patterns are more complex, smaller areas are marked out for clearing or new planting.

It is possible to see how these imaginative policies are already transforming Ennerdale as one walks through the forest towards the head of the lake. The most obvious and striking fact is how varied and pleasant a forest walk can be. Not very far below Black Sail Hut there is a clear area, where a wide platform has been created sloping quickly away to the River Liza. Here is a dear little wooden marker post, pointing across the river to the immense, not to say terrifying, mountain mass on the other side, inscribed merely "Pillar". You will be all right as far as the matchstick footbridge, but then you will be on your own, the gentle stroll will be at an end. Pillar would not be out of place among the Black Cuillin of Skye. Its terrible jagged skyline darkens even a bright May afternoon, and Pillar Rock, protruding above that skyline, casts its own shadow over the high rugged cwm below which the naked buttresses fall away vertically to the forest fringe.

The other side of the valley is bleak enough to be sure, but the flanks of High Stile and Red Pike cannot compare with Pillar. The plantations even manage to claw their way high

Alex Gibson, warden, Black Sail Youth Hostel

into the stony wilderness. Probably they always were ragged and irregular in outline up there; anyway, they do succeed in softening the intimidating bareness. Much of the higher planting is spruce - the ends of all the twigs a delightfully delicate shade of green in the springtime, all the brighter by contrast with the more sombre aspect of the older growth.

Farther down the dale the original cover of conifers was partially relieved many years ago by a screen of hardwoods, mainly beech but interspersed with laburnums! The young beech leaves shine like water as they reflect the strong sunlight. The trees were not so closely planted as to cut out the more distant prospect; looking back to Windy Gap, there is a glimpse of Great Gable behind the nearer bulk of Kirk Fell. But it is Pillar that presides over upper Ennerdale - so near, so high, so steep and rocky. Few places in Lakeland match its fierce wildness. Somehow it is not a benign presence, and one is glad to move into the orbit of the lake, now coming into sight below Anglers' Crag.

This walk through the forest is unique in the dales. Since there are very few sheep, the conifers and the birches have begun to seed themselves wherever there is enough light and a little soil. In the cleared areas many broadleaved trees have recently been planted as well. With time, as the different groupings of trees establish themselves in relation to each other, and to the open glades already forming above the road, there will be an approximation to the ancient tree-covered aspect of the dales. Meanwhile, in the absence of motor traffic, there is, as one nears the lake at Gillerthwaite, something of the atmosphere that prevailed everywhere until the coming of the car. It is so quiet - apart from the murmuring Liza, the only sounds are of tiny birds and, in May, the call of the cuckoo mingling with the distant cry of lambs. The scent of hawthorn added to the fresh woodland perfume makes an intoxicating contrast to the ambience of most valley roads today.

As the road accompanies the shining Liza for the final stretch before the lake, we pass some of the genuinely older woodland, twisted oaks covering the huge boulders that deterred even the Forestry Commission from trying to plant anything. This ancient woodland, which has been designated a Site of Special Scientific Interest, forms the background to the path along the southern margin of the lake. It is purely a footpath, and a stony one at that, crossing stream after little stream that has come snaking through the oak and birch that cling to the steep fellside. Ennerdale Water now forms the foreground to a more open prospect. The mountains that separate us from Buttermere leap along the skyline above the forest that we have left behind. Nearer Anglers' Crag the oak scrub peters out, and the path begins to climb. At one point we are reminded vividly of the industrial associations of the valley, as the dark scoriae of an iron bloomery site mark the way. The redness of the soil is plain in several places. Then follows a quite sporting section of path, across the face of Anglers' Crag, before the stroll down to the unobtrusive dam and waterworks buildings at the foot of the lake.

However, splendid though this walk has been, we have not seen half of Ennerdale Water and its surroundings. In no other Lakeland valley is there such a startling and abrupt contrast between the wildness above, and the pastoral charm below, the lake. A footpath follows the shore right round to Bowness Knott, where it joins the broad forestry road from Black Sail. On the left are fertile meadows, trees and hedges, farms and cultivation; on the right is the lake and its encircling mountains. When the indefatigable Edwin Waugh came here in 1882 he stayed at the now vanished Boathouse Inn, situated above this path. It was a wild October night, with moonshine breaking through storm clouds, and he took

Ennerdale - Pillar and the River Liza

a boat on to the lake, after a warning from the landlord not to venture far out. He was rewarded with a scene of Wagnerian splendour. One minute the fells *were lit up to their summits by the moon; the next, they were all in gloom, and half concealed by drifting mists.* The following morning he proposed walking to Buttermere over Scarth Gap, but first he asked the landlady a rather silly question - Where could he get a shave? After the boat episode she must have thought "We've got a right one here", and replied drily that he needn't be particular about his chin, and that he would be more likely to need a shoemaker than a barber; adding, for good measure, that if he were benighted on Scarth Gap, and then mistook his way, finding himself back at the Boathouse, they would find a bed for him.

Mrs Linton, twenty years before Waugh, symbolised this contrast between wildness and settled farming by her description of how the lower slopes above Mireside were dotted every summer and autumn by hundreds of beehives, brought thither on carts from miles around: *for the bees to get strength and sustenance before winter time.* Mireside Farm, the last one before the forest in the dark shadow of Bowness Knott, is one of the many National Trust farms in the Lake District, and illustrates well the key role which the trust plays in maintaining the fragile balance between preserving the landscape and taking advantage of up-to-date farming techniques.

One of the most difficult problems facing the dales farmer is the proper care of his watercourses, walls and hedges; this is very time-consuming, and the labour force is seldom larger than the farmer himself and possibly a grown-up son. The National Trust estate teams are able to provide essential support in seeing that this kind of work is kept up. Indeed, they go further, and undertake what can only be described as landscape maintenance. Basically, the drainage sikes on the higher fells slopes have to be kept clear and confined within their proper channels; wall gaps, created by frost and rain or the feet of scrambling sheep, have to be repaired (who has not seen the temporary job consisting of an iron bedstead and baler twine, fixed up twenty years ago?) and hedges need regular layering to keep them stock-proof and provide shelter from the weather. National Trust farms like Mireside are distinguished by the way that attention to these matters is no more than the start.

Footpaths over the farmland are kept in good repair, and groups of trees are planted here and there, to provide shelter or simply for their long-term visual and ecological contribution to the total landscape. A visitor may see this work in progress wherever the trust maintains a presence in any of the dales - a length of traditional cobble wall being rebuilt, a dyke under construction for the planting of a hedge. The completed dyke, made from big, rough stones and earth, will then be protected by temporary fences until the mixture of hedging trees can look after themselves; hawthorn principally, but including a scattering of blackthorn, and the occasional rowan or ash which will be allowed to grow into a tree. One visit to Mireside coincided with the presence of a small group of young men learning how to lay cobblestones, as they relaid a section of the old farmyard. No farmer could begin to do with his own resources the work which the trust undertakes. In the early 1990s a project to construct or replace ten miles of hedges in the Ennerdale area is under way, at a cost (1990 prices) of over £12 per metre. This work is not intended to fossilise the landscape, but to perpetuate its diverse attractiveness while at the same time providing the framework within which the farmer can do his job more efficiently.

From Mireside in one direction it is only a few minutes' walk to the wilderness whither

Above:
Ennerdale Water and Anglers' Crag

Left:
Bill Barker and trainee. YTS Direct Training path improvement near Bowness Knott

the unshaven Edwin Waugh set his face, though the people who lived at Gillerthwaite, at the head of the lake, must surely have resented such exaggerated descriptions as the more imaginative early travellers chose to apply. In the other direction, we may walk by well-tailored hedges, enclosing beautifully kept fields. There are one or two surprises, maybe. One wonders what John Littledaile of Routen, who was fined five shillings in 1673 by the manor court "for cutting down of wood withot a lycence", would have to say about the llamas currently to be seen grazing the Routen pastures. He would not have been taken aback, however, by the sight of a person walking a couple of hounds along the road unless, perhaps, he stopped to chat. Even so, we cannot be certain that he would not have known they were trail hounds, because the origin of this Lakeland sport is unknown. It could well be that as early as the seventeenth century the dalesmen were wont to exercise some of their foxhounds during the summer by pitting them one against another in pursuit of an aniseed trail.

What is certain, is that today hound trailing is quite distinct from foxhunting and engrosses the interest of a great many people in the dales. One of the most important of the hundreds of fixtures that take place in a season is the one held at Kirkland Leaps, above the western end of Ennerdale. A person does not need a lot of capital or specialised equipment to keep two or three trail hounds, and if one of them is a bitch that produces a good litter, there may be the expectation of a small profit. Not that anyone would interest themselves for the sake of making money - prizes at the meets are extremely modest. The rewards are in the approbation and esteem of the cognoscenti, and in the business of training these remarkably likeable beasts.

As a beginner, you should buy your puppy in, say, March. This is an advantage because January 1 each year is the official birthday of puppies born during that calendar year. By September your puppy will be big enough to start training. First, he must learn to follow you. Next, you need the help of a friend who holds the dog. You now put a trail rag on the floor in front of him, show him a biscuit and walk away slowly, calling his name. At this point the friend looses him, and he will follow you - probably. This is repeated until the lesson is learned but it is merely stage one. Gradually, you lengthen the distance and make the exercise more complicated. He has to come over a wall, and round a bend. Soon, with luck, he is ready to run a little trail. The friend shows him where the scent starts, and off he goes. Meanwhile you are waiting somewhere out of sight with food, and when he appears you call his name loudly. So far, so good. But this is merely a dead-end trail. Now he must learn the real thing. A trailer (maybe the helpful friend - and there are a lot of husband and wife teams in the sport) walks towards your puppy, dragging a scent. He must now go past the trailer, pick up the scent and follow it away from the trailer. It is at this stage that a few puppies fail; others get the idea only after tuition from an older hound. Finally, by November say, you are ready to begin earnest trailing, increasing the length of the trail bit by bit, perhaps eight minutes by Christmas, working up to the statutory twenty to twenty-five minutes for the start of the next season. All of this, of course, explains why most trail hound owners look pretty healthy. They go on getting a lot of exercise themselves, because when you have trained your puppy you need to walk him for several miles every day.

For many years now, hound trailing has been very closely organised. Your puppy will have a name you use familiarly - Dash, perhaps - by which you will call him at home and

Top left;
Hound trail in progress,
Ennerdale Show

Centre left:
Hound trail followers A. Rudd
and John Sanderson enjoying the
sun before the racing starts

Below:
Dennis Crone and helper await
the hound trail finish

as the field comes in at the end of the trail: but you also register his official kennel name with the Hound Trailing Association, just as they have to do for racehorses. There is less formality about the actual trail meetings. You can just turn up with your puppy on the day. For his first year he will be restricted to entering puppy trails, which must last for a minimum of fifteen minutes, and are usually won and lost in just over twenty. A senior trail, to be valid, must last for twenty-five minutes, and generally the first dogs will have completed the eight miles or so of the course in about half an hour.

There you are then, your puppy getting all excited by the presence of the other dogs, the spectators and the noisy bookmakers. You glance nervously at the blackboards to see whether you are much of a fancy. The trailer is already approaching with his rag. The timekeeper is fingering his watch. You are all lined up, straining for the slip. A course official moves along the line, counting the number of entries and putting a dab of colour on the shoulder of each hound - not that anyone would dream of trying to substitute a runner at a quiet spot half way round, not these days. They used to, of course. Unless it is one of the favoured places like Wasdale Head where you can watch the field panting right round the trail, you now have to be content with an occasional sighting through your binoculars until the sound of many hounds giving mouth announces that the end is nigh. "Dash! Dash!!!" you cry frantically amid the enveloping uproar, and beat his food dish with a spoon, as if he could pick out this separate strand in the general cacophony.

It is the normal thing to have a meal waiting for the competitors at the conclusion of each trail. In fact, during the season, your average trail hound lives pretty well. Hound meal is the basis, though some owners like to use greyhound racing food - and you can see why when you look at a clipped hound at his mid-season peak. He resembles a greyhound much more than his foxhunting cousin. You can give your puppy meat or fish (but not red meat if the weather is hot), or vegetables. Plenty of liquid is advisable, and this may take the form of milk and eggs. But don't include fat or salt in his diet. If you bring up your puppy on good quality food, he will repay you by his additional stamina when he grows up. And a trail is a real test of a hound's fitness. He is running faster than one mile every four minutes, usually over difficult ground. The trailer, of course, is careful to avoid dangerous places but even so, pads can be cut on sharp stones or blistered when the ground is baked in hot weather. The most serious hazard is from scratches or bruises caused by the headlong scramble over wire fences or stone walls - the sight of a trail leaping over a wall must be one of the most exhilarating in any sport.

Meanwhile, setting aside the distraction of hound trails, the best way of getting to Ennerdale Bridge from Routen is to walk. The metalled road runs through Croasdale, a tiny hamlet which somehow seems to have been left stranded when John Littledaile's lifestyle passed away; but there are flowery byways too, where glimpses of the lake beckon back to the shore-line path. This is a delightful place to sit, watching the cloud shadows move slowly over the face of the hills. For company we have a ewe and her grown-up lamb, drifting rather aimlessly among the trees. One of the farmers chances this way presently, in shirt-sleeves, moving briskly and accompanied by three dogs; an elderly black and white one, strictly to heel, a black youngster, charging all over the place, and a brown and white worker, who disappears after a quiet word from the boss, and returns in a moment escorting our two sheep on their way now to rejoin the flock.

We are not far from the Boathouse Inn, where Waugh made himself look foolish, but today the handiest source of refreshment is in Ennerdale Bridge, a short distance below the lake foot, through more forestry plantations. There really is a bridge, a handsome one over the River Ehen (née Liza before her union with the lake). Leaning over the parapet, we look into a deep pool with 'fish' written all over it, overhung with alder and ash. It is a working village, rather than a collection of props set out to furnish a tourist trap, and linked as a dormitory with British Nuclear Fuels Limited more than with the coach tour operators. The houses are of many periods and styles, some of them white and shining in a distinctly un-Wordsworthian mode, yet all blending harmoniously. The village school gives off an aura of learning and an aroma of chips in equal measure. The village church, down a little lane just over the bridge, does not trade upon its admittedly tenuous link with Wordsworth. The building that the poet knew has been replaced by what the official guidebook kindly describes as a church which "although Victorian in date...is discreet in style and entirely in scale with its surroundings." He had used the old church as the setting for his poem *The Brothers*. Leonard, having been away from the valley as a mariner for many years, returns to seek his brother. He sees the village priest outside the church, employed along with his wife and youngest child, carding and spinning wool. In the course of the ensuing conversation, Leonard discovers that his brother is dead, having fallen from the top of Pillar Rock:

> *You see yon precipice; · it wears the shape*
> *Of a vast building made of many crags;*
> *And in the midst is one particular rock*
> *That rises like a column from the vale,*
> *Whence by our shepherds it is called THE PILLAR.*

And Leonard departs back to his seafaring, in profound sadness, not having revealed his identity.

This superb and moving poem appeared in *Lyrical Ballads*. Apart from its intrinsic merit, it reveals how far-reaching and deep was Wordsworth's knowledge and understanding of the Lake District and its inhabitants. *The Brothers* was written while he was still a young man, yet his observation and perception of the inescapable realities of life in this remote dales community leaves everyone else floundering in his wake.

The presence of Pillar and its rock in the poem is interesting, too. In the pioneering days of rock climbing in the nineteenth century this spot was supposed to be inaccessible. After records began to be kept, there was a bottle on the top into which the triumphant climber traditionally placed his visiting card. Yet in the 1790s, here was a group of local shepherds for whom this was all in a day's work:

> *He had gone forth among the new-dropped lambs,*
> *With two or three companions, whom their course*
> *Of occupation led from height to height...*

So it had always been. John Littledaile and his ancestors must have ranged over those same heights many times. The valley of Ennerdale looks up beyond the lake to the shadow of Pillar's tremendous crags: the River Ehen continues on its way to the sea through west Cumberland, by Cleator Moor and Egremont - but that is another country.

Loweswater

VII: Crummock & Buttermere

Though so closely united, they are very different in character, passing from the tame and pastoral prettiness of Loweswater through the mature grandeur of Crummock up to the stern severity of the head of Buttermere; striking a chord of beauty, unlike and yet harmonious, not to be bettered in the country.

Mrs Linton.

FROM CROASDALE it is possible to walk along the minor high-level road, more or less following the boundary of the national park by way of Lamplugh to Fangs Brow Farm. There are several advantages in doing this. Not only is the road unfrequented and the going easy, but on a clear day a wonderful wide prospect opens across west Cumberland over the sea, and out to the hills of south-west Scotland. Then from Fangs Brow, we may turn right in order to approach the Vale of Lorton via Loweswater. Most of the early writers about the Lakes were a bit patronising about Loweswater - with phrases such as the one Mrs Linton used, or: *a pleasing object during the ascent from the bridge (over Mosedale beck).* They should have come from Fangs on a bright morning in early spring when the mountain air is cold and crisp, and the March sunshine suddenly swallows up the rippling lake in a flood of dazzling silver light. A patch or two of snow remains on the low hills across the water, the whiteness matching that of the tight pussy willow catkins by the shore. Then, as we move on, the big mountains gradually line up to seal the distant view, so that at last they are crowding one another, peak by peak.

Near the foot of the lake the narrow road is partially blocked by a straggle of Land Rovers and pick-up trucks; farmers are leaning on the wall or their cab roof, binoculars trained on Mellbreak. But we are not going hunting, and take the road into the Vale of Lorton. Snowdrops are in flower along the hedge bottom - escapees from the wide drifts to be seen in all the farm gardens and orchards. In the more sheltered sections of the overgrown old hedge the thorns are showing the first suggestion of green. Not far from Thackthwaite we see that someone else is taking an interest in the hedge. An elderly man has just cut out a long straight section of wood, and is putting a little saw back into his pocket. He is one of the select fraternity of Lakeland stick makers, and has just spotted a likely piece of raw material. As we pass the time of day, he allows the information to drop that he was friendly with the legendary Arthur Irvine, of Eskdale; he confides that he seldom goes out without his saw, and that whenever an embryo stick catches his eye, he cuts it there and then, regardless of the time of year. "If you leave it, and think you'll come back, you can nivver find t'booger," he says.

Stick making is one of those ancient crafts which is in some danger of being devalued in these commercial times, but your real craftsman has his eye only on the needs of the farmers and shepherds, with a sideways glance at the stick racks on the showfields. First comes the business of combing the hedgerows for almost any piece of hardwood that is long and straight enough - hazel, blackthorn, holly, cherry, ash. Then your cutting goes to hang in the cellar for eighteen months or so. Maybe the stem will be attached to a stout section or root or branch in which the practised eye can see a handle; but more usually this part of the stick will be separate, and fashioned from horn. Here again, good relations with the prospective customers are essential, as well as long-term planning. A farmer may have had to de-horn one of his tups if the second curl of his horns has begun to grow into his eye; or he may have removed them from an aged ram before his last sad journey to the knacker's. But whatever its source, the stick maker's supply of horn will have to join his wood in storage for at least a year. If you try to use a horn too soon, you will find that after heating it tends to resume its original shape. The horn, obviously, is no good if it is hollow, but flaws caused perhaps by fights of long ago do not matter, unless the stick is being made with the showground specifically in mind.

Having selected a mature piece of wood, you have to ensure that it is perfectly straight, if necessary with the help of a little dry heat, taking care to protect the bark with kitchen foil. Then comes a preliminary light sandpapering, and a smoothing away of any knots so that they follow the line of the shank. At the top of the shank you must fashion a peg to fit into the hole which you will bore into the base of the horn handle. Now comes the really tricky part of the job - making your handle. You heat the horn gently to make it malleable, then shape it to the required curve in a vice, where you leave it, tied into this shape, overnight. This sounds easy, until you look closely at the handle of a crook, or even a simple working stick. Part of the secret is to start from the heel, or base, of the horn once you have squared it off.

But look carefully at a 'fancy' stick, which may have a pheasant or an otter carved out of the single piece of horn. There are hours of skilled work here, re-heating and using little files and chisels with delicate precision. These fancy sticks are popular with visitors, or as presentation sticks 'for best'. The writer recalls such an occasion, when the recipient's terrier and a favourite hound were plainly and individually recognisable. Your farmer, however, will nearly always go for a plain stick, in the making of which form and function come together in a finished work of art.

Back to the actual process of making a stick. The plainly shaped handle has been firmly fixed to the shank, consolidated with wood glue, and perhaps a pin of non-rusting metal; then bound with a metal ferrule. This joint between handle and shank has to be very strong - the stick may have to take the force of a ewe in full flight. Also, there has to be the width of four sizeable fingers between the nose of the handle and the shaft - the stick will be no good if it won't fit round that ewe's neck. Finally, the shaft has to be long - longer than a gentleman's walking stick, but not too long, because once you have collared your sheep, you have to be near enough to grab it with your spare hand.

Our Lorton stick maker has done a bit of judging himself, he says, and these practical considerations are uppermost in his mind as he takes each stick from the rack for appraisal. But at a show he is also looking for a good finish to the shank, and at the polish of the handle. He himself sometimes rubs with a piece of deerhorn to enhance the final shine. He checks each stick for straightness and balance (a man may be walking with it over rough ground for several hours together - it is like the balance of his bat for a test cricketer), and sees whether the nose of the handle is dead central, and level with the collar ferrule. As a final refinement, although varnishing does not disqualify a stick, some makers prefer to spend hours polishing and repolishing.

Not a vehicle has come by as we have been talking, but a whole crowd of sheep has materialised from some gap farther along the hedge. The stick maker gently ushers them back into one of the big rectangular fields that run down to the valley bottom on this side of Lorton village or, more accurately, villages. Our road brings us before long to Low Lorton. Here are friendly looking pairs of little old cottages and the Wheatsheaf Inn, white-painted walls reflecting the sunlight; the window surrounds and plinth black, in the same idiom as we noticed at Strands. And that, apart from the group of houses by the bridge, is Low Lorton. The River Cocker swings away through broad fields, a wide stream rippling over its pebbly bed. A short distance below the bridge we notice an odd feature, that there are at least three places where easy access for a cart to reach the water has been created in the fairly distant past. They are certainly not fords, or stances for fishermen. Possibly they mark the spots where flax was brought to the river for retting when the vale was much more industrial than it is today. In the middle of the nineteenth century considerable quantities of flax were produced around Lorton. Mr M.Davies-Shiel, the Lake District historian, discovered, for example, that one of the fields near Thackthwaite was called "Hemplin". The retting process consisted of soaking the long stems until it was possible to detach the fibres which could be spun once they had dried. Further inquiry leads to the discovery that one of the innocent-looking houses by the bridge was formerly a corn-mill; the present idyllic atmosphere of the place is in complete contrast to its busy workaday past.

Saint Cuthbert's Church stands in the parkland associated with Lorton Hall, midway between the two portions of the village, and very handy for the squire. It is light and airy, and unusual among Lakeland churches in being built in the Georgian 'gothick' style, a late example, dating from the 1820s. The greater part of High Lorton faces the park, but is made to keep its distance by the high stone park wall - except opposite one cottage, where it has been lowered, and the gap filled with old-fashioned iron railings. The name of the cottage? Park View. One would love to know the views of everyone else in the village when this little

Loweswater and Mellbreak

favour was granted from the hall! We may be reasonably certain that it wasn't granted to any of the Wesleyans whose plain little chapel, dated 1840, stands close by.

This was the time of Lorton's greatest prosperity, from which many of the well-proportioned, tidy cottages must surely date. Like the Wheatsheaf Inn, their window surrounds are painted black, or sometimes ochre; and like the church, their walls are cement-rendered, with rustication lines in white or cream. Nearer to Boon Beck there is a remarkable row of cottages, each with eight steps up to its porch and doorway. Behind these cottages is an old mill, partly built out over supporting columns in the stream, and steps have been built down to the water here. Crossing Boon Beck, a clear, bright stream, tumbling with glorious irresponsibility over its native bedrock, we come to two lots of tenters' cottages (the map tells us this is Tenter Lane); below the bridge is another large, dour, industrial-looking building. In short, High Lorton is a treasure house of industrial archaeology, unrivalled in the Lake District.

'Tenter' gives the first clue - and indeed, there was a fulling mill as well as a flax mill here. The specialist can point to the level platforms in the fields, where the woollen cloth was stretched on tenterhooks to dry. The flax mill, of which only the foundations remain, together with the head race and pit for its water-wheel, was built in 1837 and continued in production, it seems, until about 1940. The builder was John Jennings, and now we quote from Mannex and Whelan's 1847 *Cumberland Directory: At High Lorton is a flax-spinning and thread manufactory, belonging to John Jennings, jun.; and a brewery belonging to John Jennings and Co.* High Lorton is, in fact, the original home of the famous brewery. The big building below the bridge was probably the vat house; the other brewery buildings are the ones behind the cottages with the steps, which housed some of the Jennings workforce. The reason why the ground floor of the cottage was given over to storage, rather like some of the old fishermen's houses on the Fife coast, is not obvious. The real enthusiast will have difficulty in getting away from the Vale of Lorton, because there are traces of tanyards yet to be seen, iron bloomeries, and mills, including a thresh mill at Scales, higher up the road from Boon Beck bridge.

However, industrial archaeology is not the sole reason for lingering here. The vale of the Cocker has always been one of the richest and best-favoured of the Lakeland dales. As long ago as 1797 William Hutchinson could write in his *History of Cumberland* that the area round Lorton is *beautified with rich meadows, eminences covered with wood, and scattered hamlets.* The farmers grew all sorts of grain, turnips and potatoes; their sheep, horses and black cattle were larger than average. But Hutchinson's comment leads on to a further point. From the earliest days when eighteenth century writers began to expound the principles by which the quality of a landscape should be judged, the Vale of Lorton has been accorded a very high rating. William Gilpin, apostle of the picturesque, may serve as spokesman for the rest: *Nature, in this scene, lays totally aside her majestic frown, and wears only a lovely smile. The Vale of Lorton is of the extended kind, running a considerable way between mountains, which range at about a mile's distance. They are near enough to screen it from the storm, and yet not so impending as to exclude the sun... Except the mountains, nothing in this scenery is great; but every part is filled with those sweet engaging passages of Nature, which tend to soothe the mind and instil tranquillity.*

Except the mountains... They have shown themselves as a dark silhouette whenever we have been able to tear ourselves away from the tanyards, or the *variegated scene* (Mannex

Grasmoor reflected in Crummock Water

again.) Another narrow road takes us peacefully enough towards the foot of Crummock Water, by Hope Beck, from which we may look down on the valley, its long-established pattern of walls and hedges enclosing the fields where (most!) of the sheep are grazing. We could get sidetracked again in the area between Loweswater and Crummock, from Brackenthwaite to tiny Loweswater village; indeed it is advisable at the height of the holiday season to use these minor roads, then walk to the upper portion of the valley using the footpath below Mellbreak. But on a fresh March day, after heavy rain overnight, the main road is not busy, and much drier. It bounces along under the precipitous slopes of Grasmoor, whence unbridled screes fan out onto the brackeny common which runs down to the road.

On the other side is the fell wall, bounding the better quality land. From the far side of the lake the faint sound of hounds in full cry floats across the dark water. Sure enough, there they are, a moving line of pale specks, vanishing into a gully then reappearing to race across the breast of Scale Knott in the sunshine. The men with binoculars have moved to this road and are posted some way in front of us, but not everyone has time to stand and stare this morning. A young man is hard at work repairing a gap where the ancient wall has collapsed - perhaps weakened by the recent rains and then brought down by a scrambling sheep. He is surrounded by his raw material, as unpromising a collection of stones as could be imagined. Often the oldest walls are constructed from the rounded 'cobbles', which could be picked out of a handy beck or were simply lying on the land. In extreme situations, in Wasdale, for example, or Dunnerdale, the walls served not only as field boundaries but also as field clearance dumps. In upper Wasdale, they are enormously thick; in the Duddon Valley they are founded on colossal boulders which could only have been dragged from the projected field with infinite labour.

Our worker at Crummock has got right down to basics. For a distance of several yards he has cleared all the debris to about a foot below ground level, and is now rebuilding completely. The biggest stones have gone down here, some taking up the whole width of the foundation, easily a yard or so. The crowbar he has been using leans against the good section of wall nearby. On these big stones he is now slowly building up, making sure that there is a slight batter on each side, so that in section the finished job will be A-shaped. His experienced eye can judge which stones will match in completing this three dimensional jigsaw. That the stones are rounded is no problem to him, though sometimes he will pin them with a wedge-shaped stone from the middle, to prevent them from rocking. The middle of the wall, the hearting, is filled with small stones and rubble. Then, when he has reached approximately half the height of the finished wall, he will lay a line of flat stones as 'throughs'. These have probably been salvaged at some time from a quarry waste tip. If they are a bit too long, this doesn't matter. They can protrude from the uneven wall face without causing inconvenience to anyone except the sheep - a hungry Herdwick in search of food will tackle a seven-foot wall with every prospect of getting across. The technical reason for putting in the throughs is that they act as stabilisers. Without them, the weight of the hearting could push the wall out, because there is no mortar or cement to hold everything together. As the wall increases in height, so the average size of the stones becomes smaller. An incidental advantage of this diminishing size in the upper courses is that the waller does not have to lift the heaviest stones so far - he has to manhandle several tons during an ordinary day's work.

Sheep , Crummock

Lakeland walls make a complete study in themselves, because they vary not only according to their age, but in relation to the type of stone that is available locally. A wall of Eskdale granite would look quite incongruous in Langdale, and our wall repairer at Crummock would never dream of using Coniston slate, even if you offered to bring him a lorry-load. We asked him about some of the finer details of his craft: about the cam stones that finish off the top of the wall. Again, there are local traditions of using flat stones or rounded ones, whether you should always cam 'updyke' or not. Basically, the point is that the cams help to prevent the weather from getting into your wall and, properly maintained, they are a further deterrent to the nimble marauding sheep. Then he explained how to stop a wall for a gateway - picking out the squarer stones, or even dressing some with his big hammer. Very often a large flat stone is fixed at the top, protruding into the gateway. A vertical pin on the gate itself can pass through a hole in this stone to act as the top hinge. In many of the remoter corners of the dales, pairs of old gateposts are still to be seen. These have a row of holes cut down their middle, like waistcoat buttons, except that they are round in one post and square in the other. Ash poles, squared at one end, used to be fixed across the opening to make an effective and simple gate.

On such a bright morning, it looked like splendid healthy outdoor activity, but the waller reminded us of the times when the winter rain comes on, and you pull a sack over your shoulders, and there is no place to shelter and get a little warmer when you eat your bait, except the lee side of the wall. At least you realise at such a time how a good wall can be a life-saver for your stock, compared with a poor little post and wire fence. As we leave him now we are among the mountains, and the need for shelter is clear when we look up to Red Pike, where a snow cornice marks the skyline, or High Stile, ragged cloud hugging its summit, its rocky face seamed and cross-banded by snow-filled gullies and cracks. Yet Gilpin's words come back to us - these majestic peaks are very aptly related to the foreground. They are much more rugged than the hills round Loweswater, but not intimidating, as in upper Eskdale or below Pillar. Mellbreak has been described as Wasdale Screes in little, but again moderation breaks in; it looks quite domesticated, especially in late summer when the heather is in flower.

Good farming plays its part in maintaining the balance of this landscape: cutting your bracken regularly, burning your heather in rotation and not overstocking the high fells. Rannerdale Farm, like Mireside in Ennerdale, is one of the National Trust's showcases, illustrating how much the combination of hard work and good practice can contribute to the appearance of the dales. But it is a fiendishly difficult balancing act - these are no hobby farms kept to titillate the hordes of summer visitors whose mere presence can sometimes make the real work of the farmer almost impossible. This is the greater pity because Buttermere has always been a rich oasis in the heart of the fells, echoing Hutchinson's observations on Lorton. The name means what it says, and research by Dr Angus Winchester of Lancaster University has shown that Gatesgarth was a flourishing dairy farm 700 years ago and more. Before reaching Gatesgarth, however, the path along the far side of Crummock Water has joined our less adventurous route at Buttermere village. The great advantage of taking this other path is that only a short diversion brings us to Scale Force.

In the old days visitors could be ferried over Crummock to reach the falls without having to make too much effort. Now an often very squelchy walk from Buttermere is required, but the exertion is worthwhile especially, perhaps, in the rain. After splashing

Artist at work, Buttermere Pines

over the moor, quite suddenly you confront this dark, narrow, tree-lined cleft in the hillside. It is a secret fall, with none of the ostentatious hurly-burly of, say, Skelwith Force; just a graceful white rope of water floating down, a hundred feet or more, in a single leap.

There is no need to return directly to the car park at Buttermere. Far better, having reached the bridge, not to cross it, but to continue by the path through the woods at the base of High Stile. Buttermere is a lovely lake. Stop where the water comes swirling out, gathering momentum at the stones by the little wooden footbridge. The water of the lake is clear, revealing its shingly, stony bed. The trees round the margin are not so numerous as to be suffocating. The spring sunlight catches the pale bark of the bare ash trees, so that they contrast with the sombre groups of pines that add their own distinctive note of melancholy to the landscape. Looking right to the head of the valley, we are opposed by the broad spine of Fleetwith Pike, answering the shape of Mellbreak, now in the middle distance behind us. Very soon we come to the flat wooden bridge that crosses the beck running out of Warnscale Bottom into the lake. Here the track zigzags up to Scarth Gap and on to Ennerdale. As we think idly once more of the unshaven Edwin Waugh picking his way down, four couples of hounds that have become separated from the main pack hunt noisily right round Warnscale Bottom. When they lose the scent, they mill about the fellside like ants on a stone, until one picks up a line and they all chase off beyond Gatesgarth.

There is such a strong smell of sheep by the farm buildings here that it would be a good hound that could detect the presence of a fox. At this time of year the ewes are all gathered in the best pastures ready for lambing. If the season is harsh, they will have nibbled the grass so short that a man might whip a mouse across it. There seem to be sheep everywhere at the head of the valley. Back in Buttermere village, a somnolent group of elderly Herdwicks is blocking the exit from the car park, making the place more than ever like a child's toy village. "We'll have a house here, another there, and a farm next to it, and put the car park by the farm; the church will have to go up there, so that it can overlook the village. Now where shall we put the animals? These cows can go on the road near the church, some sheep between the farmyard and the car park, and the hens round the farm, too. Let's put some people in the car park; that man can be lacing his boots, and the lady can be picking up a rucksack." The fantasy is broken by a fearful squawking. The real tractor that has been whizzing round the next field scattering fertiliser pellets has returned to base through the car park at high speed, scattering the hens in all directions, and even those sheep have discreetly melted away.

Grasmoor from Rannerdale Knotts

Detail from a shepherd's grave? Stonethwaite churchyard

VIII: Borrowdale

Bulls cannot long be kept sane in these narrow valleys; the constantly repeated echoes of their own bellowings make them mad.

Mrs Linton

THERE IS no easy pedestrian way from Buttermere to the head of Borrowdale. For the experienced fell walker, a choice of routes runs over, or around, Haystacks, then by Windy Gap to the Sty Head track, and so to Stockley Bridge, which may conveniently be regarded as marking the head of the valley. The average person would be better advised to stay on the metalled road over Honister pass; this is a splendid walk in its own right, and has the advantage of dropping down to Seatoller, the highest settlement in the dale, from which the menfolk used to walk to their work at the precarious slate quarries cut into the crags above the pass. It is a very enclosed spot, and William Gilpin did not exaggerate much when he wrote in the 1770s: *Here, in the depth of winter, the sun never shines.*

Another advantage of the Seatoller route is that you then have to walk up to Stockley Bridge, looking into the view of the mountains beyond. It must be admitted that the initial reaction may be one of disappointment. Upper Borrowdale is a typical glaciated valley, wild and stony, but scenically not in the same league as Wasdale Head or Eskdale above Throstle Garth. Stockley Bridge, from which well trodden paths run up to Sty Head and Esk Hause, consists of a single stone span over a tiny gorge, recalling in a more desolate context, the appearance of the Duddon at Birks. Back then, to Seathwaite Farm, raising dust from the path after an unusual summer drought, which has turned all the side gullies into miniature wadis and diminished the main stream to a trickle. Nearer the farm the harshness of the landscape is softened by judicious planting - numbers of broadleaves and small stands of conifers. Far up the fellside are more spoil heaps, tiny by comparison with the ones on Honister crags. They are the remains of the ancient plumbago mines, 'wad' as it used to be known. To the locals, it was a remedy for colic or the basis of a dye; on a wider stage, exported for use in mouldings (for musket and cannon balls) and for making pencils.

More eye-catching on this September morning are the sheep, heard, however, before they are seen, also high on that same fellside. A group of shepherds is bringing down hundreds of sheep from Gillercombe. We move into the small campsite field between the farm and the river, just above the narrow wooden bridge, in order to watch. The men have seven or eight dogs to help them, but their main job has already been completed, when they were rounding up the flocks from the flanks of Great Gable and the tops above Ennerdale. Now their barking combines with the holloing of the men to keep the tide of sheep moving slowly down, with occasional forays should any stray too far from the main body. They move at a sheep's walking pace, spreading quite widely where the terrain permits. As they come nearer, we can see how they pick their steps delicately amid the boulders. The varied noise of their bleating now fills the air, and that most characteristic of Lakeland smells drifts across to us. Unobtrusively, two of the shepherds have hurried on to the river bank, for a reason which soon becomes apparent - all these sheep will have to cross the narrow wooden bridge. Naturally the ones at the front - we can see now that they are Herdwicks - stop in the middle of the bridge to admire the view. They move on only when the crash and splash of big stones hurled into the pool below startle them into further slow movement.

But the bridge merely leads to an outgang, or lonnin, into the farmyard, tightly bounded by solid stone walls. The sheep are not impressed by the prospect, especially since there is useful grass in this campsite field. Within seconds we are knee-deep in swirling sheep, and within seconds more, dogs have materialised and escorted them all back to the lonnin, which is soon packed with sheep from end to end - a regular sheep-jam because, once again, the leaders have stopped. Now as the main force of men and dogs holds back to bar any retreat, a select small force pushes through the mass to stir the leaders into movement once more. Their dog returns along the wall top as they move at last into the yard, to the pens that have been prepared for them. Here they stand quietly, while the men adjourn to the farmhouse to drink gallons of reviving tea.

We have followed them back to the yard and, leaning over the cobble wall that bounds the pens, we can see that several flocks are represented. The shepherds have been gathering from a wide area of the fells, and later will have to begin the real work. In September they separate all this year's lambs into the gimmers (females, and potential breeding stock) who will be sent during October for a winter holiday in lowland pastures, probably near the coast; and the others, mainly males who were castrated in infancy, who will go to the September sales, accompanied by those aged ewes who have come to the end of their useful breeding life. There has to be a hardening of the heart here sometimes, because a shepherd gets to know each of his flock individually, and often feels a real pang as he says goodbye. The remaining sheep will be returned to the fells for a few more weeks while the in-bye fields (the ones nearest to the farm, in the valley bottom) are shut off in the hope that the October weather may allow a bit more grass to grow before the winter.

But before they go, they will have to submit to a routine dipping to keep their fleeces free from unpleasant parasites. Nowadays the dipping is carried out in the yard; the sheep, confined by fences to move in single file, are obliged in turn to immerse themselves in a kind of disinfectant bath, which for a while overpowers even their usual natural odour. In former times the dipping consisted of a forced splash in some convenient deep pool - a perfectly preserved series of stone-walled pens may still be seen, for example, by the stream which runs down past The Bell above Coniston. After this autumn run on the fells, the sheep are brought down again in late October for the ceremony of tupping. The breeding rams, or tups, do not run with the main flock. Indeed, they live a rather cosseted life, which brings to mind that of some legendary Oriental potentate, all to ensure a good crop of lambs the following spring. Their job done, they return to semi-monastic seclusion.

The extent to which the flock now winters on the fell depends on the weather and the resources of the farm. Gone are the days when it had to fend for itself as best it could. The shepherd provides regular feed of hay, silage and those vitamin-enriched blocks or canisters that must be the ewe's tasty equivalent of Marmite; if resources allow, he will keep some lower land for grazing. As the winter progresses, the time flies by; he tries to keep up with necessary work on walls, hedges and drainage ditches, while dosing the hoggs for flukes, and giving them another dip when they return from their winter pasture (hoggs are last year's lambs). And whatever the weather, by late winter, the poorer sheep will have to be brought to the in-bye land, in the hope that there will be a bite of new grass. But March is often the severest month of the year in the Lake District, and even if it should be dry and sunny, the shepherd does not win because the grass will not be growing at the precise time that the ewes are needing all the nourishment they can get.

Lambing time is in April, or even early May, the climax of the shepherd's year, when he must patrol his maternity ward fields day and night, crook in hand, dog at heel, and needful instruments or medicines in the deep pockets of his smock. He is hoping for lots of healthy twins, which is where the Swaledales and cross-bred sheep are apt to score over the pure Herdwicks. Very soon the unsteady scraps of wool and bone fill out into the cheerful rascals that rush around the field in gangs, then almost knock their mothers sideways as they demand another feed. But a lamb's life is not all joy. Later in May they are gathered for earmarking, still the most effective way of indicating to which flock an animal belongs. The marking is done with a pair of sheep clippers, the kind used for hand-clipping later in the summer. Each flock has its own special cut. Anyone interested may see them all described and illustrated in the *Shepherd's Guide*.

This remarkable publication first appeared in 1817, printed by W.Stephen at Penrith. By means of a standard illustration it details all the sheep marks for all the Lakeland flocks opposite a written summary, which includes the farm and the farmer's name. Birketts and Wilsons dominated Borrowdale at the time. The Seathwaite flock comprised several separate stocks - a not uncommon feature as small farming units came to be amalgamated. The Windside and Gillercoom stocks had a common earmark. The lamb's left ear (its near ear) was cropped, then two long cuts made into what remained (technically, twice ritted): then the right ear (its far ear) was upper halved - ie. instead of the tip being cut right off, it was sliced half way through, then cut down from the end. Next the fleeces were marked.

Stan Edmondson, shepherd, Seathwaite,
(the wettest place in England)

The wethers (which no doubt had just undergone castration as well) were distinguished with a red stroke down the near shoulder, and another from that under the chine to the hookbone - forming a sort of letter T. Finally, with a black mark applied to the head, the little lamb could go away and play once more, when he felt well enough! Birkett's hoggs and ewes received a different pattern of red marks, and his twinters a combination of red and black stokes (twinter = two winters: female lambs who have successfully graduated to the breeding stock).

Lambs stay with their mothers into the summer, and in no time at all they have to be prepared for another shock. After a temporary separation mother reappears, almost unrecognizable after clipping. There is always the most tremendous bleating as families are reunited. Formerly clipping, like haytime, was an occasion when the neighbours rallied round and helped each other; the alternative was to hire a peripatetic gang. Old photographs show farmyards lined with men, backs to the wall, each holding a sheep in front of him with one hand, a pair of clippers in the other. Today the shepherd normally uses electrically powered clippers, with minimal assistance. These clippers can be worked closer to the skin than the older manual ones, and also enable a man to get round a fleece more quickly - though few can do more than 100 in a day without becoming cross-eyed with exhaustion. As in bringing the sheep down from the fell, the secret is to keep them calm and quiet. If you can create the right atmosphere it doesn't matter whether you stand or sit, whether the sheep keeps its back legs on the ground or reclines as if in a dentist's chair. It all looks so simple - start at the right shoulder, work along the belly and round the back leg, taking particular care round the tail; then back to the shoulders, to cut away on the other side; next, holding the head firmly but gently, round the neck, before moving gradually along the back. As the job is completed the fleece falls smoothly away, ready to be wrapped loosely into a bundle and added to the growing pile inside the barn. Meanwhile the sheep, now lighter both in colour and in weight, shakes itself and moves off.

The hope is to have all the clipping done before the grass is ready to be cut for hay, so that the sheep are on the fell again, temporarily out of the way. Not that you can just open the gate and let them go. The lambs will need dipping and, just like human babies, have to be given injections to counter possible vitamin deficiency or disease. Nor can the shepherd just leave his flock to its own devices. He has to make regular visits to the heafs where they feed, with his faithful dogs. The sheep, of course, know their own dogs, and the dogs know how to treat their sheep. Not so the visiting dogs, especially the big ones that sometimes accompany walkers. The sheep will set off in a panic, in all directions, perhaps running over the lip of a precipice or getting lost in the next valley amongst someone else's flock.

And so, when the hay has been made, the shepherd's year comes full circle. August and early September is the time when, leaving the flock (he hopes) safely grazing, he may be able to take a day off for one of the shows, even, perhaps, entering a select group of animals in some of the classes. The Borrowdale Show (called the shepherds' meet) is limited to farms in parishes adjoining Borrowdale parish, and caters principally for Herdwicks and Swaledales. It has a wonderfully pleasant and relaxed atmosphere. Everyone knows everybody else, and they have all come to enjoy a day out together.

"I only come for t'russlin," a gaunt woman is saying to her companion as they nudge

Borrowdale ashes

their way to the ropes enclosing the wrestling ring. This ancient and arcane sport is a prominent feature of all the Lakeland shows, as it was formerly of wedding celebrations and wakes. The solemn ritual which accompanies each bout certainly suggests a great antiquity. Many of the serious contestants still wear the traditional costume - white vest and long johns, with beautifully embroidered black trunks. Usually there is a full sequence of bouts, from small boys to heavyweight men. The preliminaries are always the same. The contestants shake hands. Then they adopt their stance in silence - one's chin on the other's shoulder, hands clasped behind him, right arm above, and left below, the adversary's. This sounds straightforward, but it may take some time. One wrestler may leave an arm trailing like a broken wing until he is sure he can get a comfortable grip in relation to his opponent's anatomical build. Then the referee, a bit like a rugby referee inspecting a scrum, checks that the grips are fair and correct. There is a silent pause before the bout begins and, at this point, if boys are wrestling and you turn your head away, you are likely to miss the action completely, because the bigger or more skilful lad will simply pick up his opponent and put him on to the ground, quite gently, as you would put down a fairly heavy parcel. Having repeated the gesture, he has won, taking two falls out of the possible three. The young men are just as eager as the boys. Once given the signal by the referee, they will dance about jerkily till, as often as not, they go down together in a confusion of flying limbs. This is a dogfall, if it is not clear to the referee that either wrestler can claim a clean throw. But he has an experienced eye, and again like a rugby referee awarding a try, will usually point to the winner, who gets up, shaking himself, to an accompanying patter of applause from the onlookers.

What most people have come to watch are the struggles between the heavyweights. These recall a scene straight out of Homer. Full costume is no guarantee of superior skill. Sometimes a young fellow in his working clothes, seemingly just pulled in from the ring of spectators, will best the most nicely rigged man on the field. At this level there is seldom a speedy dénouement. They manoeuvre for advantage, moving round and round in a kind of stately ballet. Then there is a sudden backheel; one is caught off balance, and down he goes. It is surprising how infrequently anyone is injured in these falls - maybe because the Lakeland weather ensures that the ground is usually soft. The two men are joined again in their stylised embrace; only the cognoscenti can really appreciate what is going on - it is rather like a long series of maiden overs in a cricket match. Then, for no obvious reason, the embrace erupts in a flurry of limbs, and someone is down again. The third deciding encounter begins after a perfunctory handshake. Perseverance, physical strength and mental alertness are now to be tested to the full, for victory really means something both to the wrestlers themselves and to their wide following in the dales.

Locked together, the pair hobbles round the ring, beads of sweat standing on their brows. Each counters the efforts of the other to catch him off balance, and at the same time seeks that tiny advantage which could bring victory - a chess grand master wondering whether he dare move a pawn up a square would appreciate the position. Always there must be a lightning reaction to match each aggressive gambit with feet or body. Still they circle. Their concentration is intense. Muscles ripple and veins stand out under the strain. The crowd falls silent. Neither will concede an inch. A sudden momentum carries them into the midst of the watchers. They return to resume their statuesque jockeying for advantage. This is a bout for the connoisseur, but it stirs the blood of the most casual

Autumn tints in Patterdale

Grisedale, with Place Fell in the background

Top left;
Start of the Senior Guides
Fell Race at Rosthwaite
Shepherds' Meet

Centre left:
Cumberland and Westmorland
wrestlers, traditionally dressed,
take hold. Rosthwaite Show

Below:
Judging the shepherds' crooks,
Rosthwaite Show

visitor, too. At last, perhaps from sheer tiredness, something snaps and they subside, probably to meet again in a week or two on another showfield, when the loser will hope to turn the tables.

The fun events at the show come at the end of the day - such as the terrier races. "Keep your dogs on t'lead," advises the master of ceremonies over the loudspeaker system: "We don't want four starters and six finishers. That upsets t'judges." Anything can happen with a group of terriers, and usually does. They may chase the rabbit-skin lure, they may go off at a tangent, or they may start to fight each other. Sometimes one may even catch the lure, and kill it all over again. Then from the fantastic to the ridiculous - the impromptu tug o'war team. "Have we got a committee man doing nowt? Just for a minute?" as somebody struggles with the huge rope. "They wrapped it up i't' dark last year, that's what's up." Eventually two teams face each other, anchor man at the back of each digging in with his enormous boots. Amid much banter from the good-humoured crowd we can hear the voice over the loudspeaker as we depart: "On my left, the Herdwick All-Stars..." Glen Tubman, doyen of Lakeland show comperes, has been in great form this afternoon. Long may he flourish, to enliven and delight us at these gatherings.

The show-cum-shepherds' meet takes place at Rosthwaite, just down Borrowdale from Seathwaite and the heart of the valley proper. It is archetypal of sheep country: flat, walled fields on the valley floor, like the ones where the show is held; then the lower fell slopes, divided into irregular enclosures, often including numbers of trees, littered with boulders or marked by outcrops of living rock; finally, the steep, open land of the high fells. The Herdwicks thrive better than any others in the conditions that normally prevail up here, although they share the fells with the Swaledales and the Rough Fell sheep. It seems appropriate, then, that they should figure in the churchyard at Stonethwaite.

Christ as the Lamb of God is an image which must have come readily to mind in this dale, and several stones have the Lamb carved at their head. One of these is from the hand of a mason who did a lot of work here during the late nineteenth century, and whose work it is worth travelling far to see. His stones are not only superbly lettered; each is decorated with a roundel containing some suitable motif with accompanying text round the circumference. There is a lily, a dove with olive branch, clasped hands, an open book and, best of all, a family of sheep (Herdwicks, without a doubt) tup, ewe and twin lambs, one sucking - the inscription: *Jesus saith, Feed my Sheep.* More than anywhere else in the Lake District perhaps, this central portion of Borrowdale still embodies that quiet self-confidence which comes from a sense of continuity, and an awareness of one's proper place in the scheme of things. For once, even Baddeley did not attempt to describe. *The tourist who is not in hot haste to scale some mighty fell,* he wrote, *or to accomplish an unheard-of number of miles in his day's walk, will linger long in this Paradise within a Paradise, where he may wander at will. Those who are in a hurry should eschew the place. It is too good for them.*

Not quite wandering at will, perhaps, but from Rosthwaite there is a path down to Grange which keeps to the western side of the valley, and avoids the motor traffic that would surely qualify for Baddeley's disapproval. This way, we climb almost to the top of Castle Crag before dropping through the woods, so it is only a short detour to the summit, where the remains of an ancient fortification may still be seen. The views from here are wonderful - back over Rosthwaite towards the dale head, and out beyond Derwentwater to Skiddaw. Nearer to hand, the sides of the valley have closed in and become steeper. This

River Derwent, Borrowdale

is the Jaws of Borrowdale, the awe-inspiring foundation for the hyperbole of early travellers: *rock riots over rock* (West) and (Gilpin) *as we edged the precipices, we everywhere saw fragments of rocks and large stones scattered about, which, being loosened by frosts and rain, had fallen from the cliffs above, and show the traveller what dangers he has escaped.*

In fact, Grange was originally a monastic grange, or farm, belonging to Furness Abbey; then became home to quarrymen and miners when the Lake District was an industrial area. A short distance along the main road above Grange is the quarry once known as Rainspot Quarry from the spotted slate that was extracted there. Now its waste heaps have been colonised by birch trees, and the National Trust has contrived a car park conveniently near the Bowder Stone. It is worth stopping to look around Grange, no less than Rosthwaite. The old part of the village merges into the landscape in a way that would have pleased Wordsworth. A flag wall separates the churchyard from the road, and at this point are the biggest kerbstones in the country - enormous blocks of slate laid lengthways. Maybe they are contemporary with the church, which is a monument to its formidable founder, Margaret Heathcote. Inside, the barrel-vaulted roof is divided into sections by stone arches bizarrely cut into restless and menacing sharp teeth. This feature is repeated above the first floor windows of the dark stone house over the field named Castle Crag, which the same lady had built for the parson. In addition to founding the church, in the middle of the nineteenth century, she established a village school, at which she taught. This must have been quite an experience for the local children, because she was very definite in her principles - making her stately progress in the rain, a piece of sponge fitted to the tip of each rib on her umbrella to catch the drips, she expected not ribaldry, but curtsies or a touch of the forelock from all she met. It is not surprising to learn from the 'guide' to the Borrowdale churches, that in the eleven years for which she had patronage of the living, there were seven incumbents!

Derwentwater fills the lower portion of Borrowdale, and provides a restful conclusion to a walk from Seathwaite. By sailing to Keswick from the jetty near Grange, we can see all the encircling hills in comfort. North from Lodore, where the famous falls have cascaded down from the hanging valley of Watendlath, are Falcon Crag and Walla Crag, fearsome vertical walls of rock which may have been the source of Gilpin's apprehension of sudden death. On the western side of the lake the fells are grassy - delightful Catbells running on to Maiden Moor. As with Watendlath, the woods below Catbells bring Hugh Walpole to mind. This area is notable because it was the first Lake District property to be acquired (in 1902) by the newly formed 'National Trust for Places of Historic Interest or Natural Beauty'. The woods were bought with money raised by public subscription and declared inviolable. For Canon H.D.Rawnsley, Vicar of Crosthwaite, Keswick, and one of the three founders of the trust, it must have been particularly gratifying to see a long-cherished dream brought to reality so near his own home.

Its deciduous woodlands, some of them very old, are one of the chief glories of Borrowdale. Some, like the National Trust's Johnny Wood, on the way to Seatoller, are designated Sites of Special Scientific Interest on account of their value to specialist students - of ferns and liverworts for example. But for the ordinary person their value is in the visual impact of the trees through the changing seasons, the sounds of the birds and smells of the vegetation; above all, in the peace and calm that they enshrine. Farther north again, in the Lingholm estate, open to the public, is a different kind of woodland. Here the

Rowing boats, Derwentwater, Keswick

grounds have been imaginatively planted with a great variety of trees, but especially with masses of rhododendrons and azaleas which flourish in this damp climate on the acid soil.

From Nichol End near Lingholm the boat crosses the lake to its base at Keswick. From the landing stage it is only a few yards to Friar's Crag, most celebrated (and justly) of all Lakeland viewpoints, where there are memorials to both Canon Rawnsley and John Ruskin, who inspired his vision of the National Trust. Keswick itself has long been the focus of the northern part of the Lake District: as an industrial centre when the German miners came in the sixteenth century to exploit the copper veins at Newlands; as a literary centre when Southey lived at Greta Hall; as a crafts centre when Marion Twelves set up her Ruskin lace and linen industry in the late nineteenth century; and, for over 200 years, as a holiday centre without equal in the area.

When the Lake District was first 'discovered' round about the time when Wordsworth was born, Keswick was the place for which most discerning visitors headed, and so it has been ever since, despite the continuing assaults of opportunist commercialism. Not that our own times can outstrip the flair and inventiveness of the earliest entrepreneurs, who had the advantage that they were not dealing with mass tourism, and so could hardly wreck the environment they were exploiting by the massive scale of their activities. Peter Crosthwaite, a local man who had retired from service at sea in the fleet of the East India Company, established a museum in the town as a centre of interest and occupation for visitors on the regular wet days. According to his advertisement bill of 1792, the museum consisted of "many Hundred Natural and Artificial Curiosities from every Quarter of the world". Admittance for Ladies and Gentlemen was one shilling each; Country people, sixpence each. (How could he be sure of distinguishing?) He also sold those beautiful and accurate maps of the Lakes, executed by himself, which now change hands at high prices whenever they come on the market. He had a good eye for what would meet the needs or engage the attention of visitors: for example, it was he who devised a graded zigzag path to the top of Latrigg, from which may be seen the finest mountain panorama in the kingdom, and he arranged for the construction of the first beacon on Skiddaw summit.

Crosthwaite worked with another enterprising character in presenting extraordinary 'regattas' on Derwentwater. Joseph Pocklington owned one of the four islands on the lake - the one near Friar's Crag now known as Derwent Isle, on which he had built an imitation chapel which was really a boathouse, a pseudo-church, a stone circle modelled on the one at Castlerigg, and a fort complete with battery. At regatta time, for the entertainment, evidently, of thousands of visitors, Crosthwaite led an assault on 'Pocklington's Island', to the accompaniment of cannon fire which reverberated (it was alleged) as far away as Appleby. But let the *Cumberland Pacquet* take up the tale with its account of the regatta held on September 6, 1782.

> At eight o'clock in the morning, a vast concourse of ladies and gentlemen appeared on the side of the Derwent lake, where a number of marquees, extending about 400 yards, were erected for their accommodation. At twelve, (Query: whatever did they do all morning, after getting up so soon?) such of the company as were invited by Mr. Pocklington, passed over, in boats, to the island which bears his name; and, on their landing, were saluted by a discharge of his artillery. This might properly be called the opening of the Regatta; for as soon as the echo of this

discharge had ceased, a signal gun was fired, and five boats, which lay upon their oars...instantly pushed off the shore and began the race.

A view from any of the attendant boats...presented a scene which beggars all description. The sides of the hoary mountains were clad with spectators, and the glassy surface of the lake was variegated with a number of pleasure barges, which, tricked out in all the gayest colours, and glittering in the rays of the meridian sun, gave a new appearance to the celebrated beauties of this matchless vale.

...About 3 o'clock, preparations were made for the sham attack on Pocklington's Island. The fleet (consisting of several barges, armed with small cannon and musquets) retired out of view, behind Friar's Crag, to prepare for action;...(A truce was offered and rejected)...soon after, the fleet was seen advancing, with great spirit, before the batteries, and instantly forming in a curved line, a terrible cannonade began on both sides, accompanied with a dreadful discharge of musquetry. This continued for some time, and being echoed from hill to hill, in an amazing variety of sounds, filled the ear with whatever could produce astonishment and awe...

After a severe conflict, the enemies were driven off from the attack, in great disorder... The fleet, after a little delay, formed again, and, practicing a variety of beautiful manoeuvres, renewed the attack. Uproar again sprung up...

The garrison at length capitulated, and the entertainments of the water being finished, (towards the evening) the company moved to Keswick; to which place, from the water's edge, a range of lamps was fixed, very happily disposed, and a number of fire-works were played off.

An assembly room (which had been built for the purpose) next received the ladies and gentlemen, and a dance concluded this annual festivity...

To those whom nature's work alone can charm, this spot will, at all times, be viewed with rapture and astonishment; but no breast, however unsusceptible of pleasure, can be indifferent to that display of every beauty which decks the ancient vale of Keswick on a Regatta day.

It all sounds so much more leisurely than the busy coming and going that is the mark of today's holiday crowds. The Victorian railway town, and more recent development to provide residential accommodation and services for the multitudes of car-borne visitors, have all but obliterated the little town where Pocklington lorded it in his day. His regatta, one feels, would get short shrift from the Planning Board. One small link survives from those seemingly innocent times, which we can see as we leave Keswick. Going by Fitz Park, we may call in at the museum and look at Crosthwaite's musical stones. Then if we were feeling energetic, we could use his footpath over Latrigg, as the first stage on the way to Threlkeld, the starting point for our journey through the Vale of St John.

Window, Wythburn church

IX: Vale of St John and Thirlmere

If it is a still day, Thirlmere lies absolutely unrippled; the reflection so entire that you cannot, at first sight, tell where the line of water begins, and what is real and what is only repetition.

Mrs Linton.

THRELKELD is not really in the Vale of St John, but it is from here that the best view of the vale is to be had. Ideally you should have walked from Keswick, if not over Latrigg, then through Brundholme Woods and climbed up the bridleway to Wescoe, where the sturdy farmhouses would be much photographed if they were nearer to the main lines of communication. From the minor road which leads to Threlkeld, you can look right up to the head of the vale. An uncertain winter afternoon is a good time to be here. Helvellyn, half-hidden by masses of low heavy cloud, suggests a more tremendous grandeur than a clear day can ever reveal; there is a brightness in the sky beyond Keswick, and from the breaks in the cloud, sheets of golden light stream down to fill the valley floor.

Probably few visitors spare more than a passing thought for Threlkeld as they hurtle along the A66 - just a glimpse of a rather workday-looking village, with a decidedly unsympathetic-sounding name. This is a mistake. The dignified old church alone is worth turning aside to see. It is a spacious eighteenth century rebuild of a much older place of worship, tactfully restored early in the present century with advice from Canon Rawnsley. Members of the congregation can steal a glance through the plain round-headed windows either down to that wonderful mountainscape enclosing the vale or up to the dark, threatening south face of Blencathra, only a few yards away, it seems. No doubt in times past some of the older men let their minds wander to the days when they had traversed those fellsides in rain and shine, for reasons totally unconnected with their presence at evensong. In the churchyard stands an extraordinary monument, square in section, capped by a huge rough stone, and inscribed round the top:

Around them stand the old familiar mountains.

Fuller explanation follows:

A few friends have united to raise this stone in loving memory of the undernamed, who in their generation were noted veterans of the chase, and most of whom lie buried in this churchyard.

Forty-five names of these running huntsmen are listed, with their ages. To judge by the number who lived into their eighties, following the hunt kept them pretty fit. There is no specifically Christian wording on the memorial; the inscription round the base harks back to a romanticised and no doubt largely imaginary golden age:

The finest music is to hear the hounds
Rend the air and with a lusty cry
Awake the drowsy echo and confound
Their perfect language in a mingled voice.

But there is more to Threlkeld than this. We are in the Cumberland part of the Lake District, so the old houses have their dressed stone window surrounds painted in strong colours. Most of the nineteenth century buildings have a forbidding air, created by the heavy dark stone - like the school, dated 1849, and the Mission Room, still with a "Wayside Pulpit" notice outside, 1855. Obviously, hunting was not the sole occupation of the inhabitants and, in fact, Threlkeld was an important lead mining and quarrying centre. South, over the broad shallow valley, on the slope of Threlkeld Knott, at the very foot of the Vale of St John, are the granite quarries. These are some of the biggest quarries in the Lake District, and now that they have closed work is in progress to establish on their site a Museum of Lakeland Mines and Quarries. Above the empty levels, jackdaws swirl about the restless, jagged rock face, calling noisily to one another. Since granite breaks differently from slate, there are none of the smooth slabs which characterise the abandoned workings at Tilberthwaite, for example, or in Borrowdale. A hundred years ago the Threlkeld quarries produced vast quantities of flags and setts to pave the streets of our northern industrial towns. Later, it was found that the granite was particularly suitable for making high-grade tarmacadam. The imaginative plans of the Lakeland Mines and Quarries Trust now envisage (among many other things) that the old mineral railway here should be reconstructed to take visitors round the extensive museum site, and that there should be a museum trail, linking geological and ecological features of interest.

Working quarries in the Lake District are now restricted to the Coniston and Langdale valleys, and are almost all controlled by one big organisation. The slate is extracted by open cast methods, and the reduction of the rock to decorative slabs, walling stone or roofing slates is carried out as far as possible by machinery. Rivers to split the slabs into slates and dressers to shape them, are still needed, but they are no longer to be found at work in crude stone shelters on the nearest level ground to the quarry face. The workforce is concentrated at the largest quarry of all, near Kirkby-in-Furness just outside the Lake District. The quarrymen, therefore, figure far less prominently in the social structure of the valleys than in former times, and many a former quarryman's house has become a neat little holiday retreat or retirement home.

The discerning walker, on leaving Threlkeld, will use the pleasant byways through Shundraw to reach Saint John's Church, in the centre of the dale. This route has the advantage of permitting an easy detour to the Castlerigg Stone Circle, concerning which more nonsense has been written than about any other place in the Lake District. Certainly, the site is dramatic; the silent stones evoke a mysterious, unknowable past, but it is not more evocative than the tiny secluded church. It seems secluded now because the motor road runs along the eastern edge of the vale, directly below the quarries. In fact it is placed so as to be equally convenient for the farmers both of St John's and Naddle. It is difficult for visitors today to think of Naddle as a small, distinct valley now that a dual-carriageway highroad cuts through it, but a glance at the map will show that the church is on the saddle of ground connecting the two vales. A conversation with any of the farmers will put us right, too. Naddle is "ovver t'hill" if you live in St John's Vale, and vice versa.

The tiny ancient well in the churchyard could easily predate the stone circle as a focus for faith and piety. The meticulously lettered gravestones tell something of those who have lived and worshipped here more recently, like John Wren of Birkett Bank, who died in 1784. At the head of the stone is his family crest, surmounted by a hound moving purposefully forward. John would have been at ease with any of those forty-five commemorated up at Threlkeld. Another John was John Richardson, born at Piper House, Naddle, in 1817, marrying Grace Birkett of City House, Wythburn, in 1841, becoming village schoolmaster in 1858, and living in the valley until he died at Bridge House in 1886. There is a small exhibition inside the church in honour of Richardson, who ought to be better known.

He wrote a quantity of verse in the local dialect, which equals that of many more celebrated poets who habitually use the common speech of their locality. He knew the people better than Wordsworth did, and occasionally is able to depict their outlook and way of life in a way that brings to mind Samuel Laycock, or even Burns. He wrote in the language of the Cumberland farmers - it was his own speech - catching the idiom and the rhythm. A *Grummel or a Grean* begins:

> *It's grummel! grummel! grummel!*
> *Fra' mwornin' still till neet.*
> *Fra ya week entill t'udder*
> *Theer's nivver nowt 'at's reet.*

We have all met folk like this grumbler:

> *If t'sun shine het i' summer,*
> *Befwore a week's geàn ower,*
> *Aw things 'ill be clean burnt up,*
> *Withoot theer comes a shooer.*
> *An' if it rains i' hay-time,*
> *It's sek a desperat keàse,*
> *T' rain-cloods ur nowt for blackness*
> *To t'clouds theer on his feàce.*

- or like Jobby Dixon who "lik'd his beer" and on the morning after the night before

Castlerigg Stone Circle

couldn't face the "poddish" that his wife set before him for breakfast, or a cup of tea, or a posset of milk and good wheat bread. Finally:

> *Auld Betty steùd a bit, an' then*
> *She gev a wink at me;*
> *An' then she sed, 'I dunnet know,*
> *I doot thoo's gan to dee;*
> *What, can't 'e tak a glass o' rum?*
> *Thoo'll mannish that, I's warn.'*
> *'Wy, fetch me yan, 'auld Jobby sed,*
> *'I mun hev summet, barn.'*

Richardson's themes relate to the situations that recur eternally in people's lives: the heir who runs through his inheritance, young love, the old widower. His style rings true to life; there is no attempt at fine writing, no condescension to the dialect, no romanticising of the situation (as, it must be said, Wordsworth was apt to do). He catches the physical environment, as well as the quirky, knotty people, as John Clare had done. In *What used to be Lang Sen* an old man recalls the past and Richardson, without comment, shows us the weakness and limitations of his outlook, at the same time as he engages our sympathies, as effectively as the Roman poet ever did when he reflected on the fugitive passage of time.

> *I's grou'en feckless, auld, an' leàmm,*
> *My legs an' arms ur far fra' t'seàmm,*
> *As what they use to be:*
> *My back oft warks, an's seldom reet;*
> *I've sceàrse a teùth to chow me meat,*
> *An' I can hardly see.*
>
> *Bit yance I cud ha' plew't or sown,*
> *Or shworn my rigg, or thick gurse mown,*
> *Wi' enny man alive:*
> *An' yance, when in t'Crowpark we ran,*
> *(An' theer war some 'at cud run than,)*
> *I com in t'furst o' five.*
>
> *At russelin', if I say't mysel,*
> *Theer wassent menny cud me fell,*
> *An' theer war gooduns than:*
> *I've russel't oft wi' Gwordie Urn,*
> *An' still cud fell him in my turn,*
> *An' he was neah bad man.*
>
> *An' who wi' me cud follow t'hoonds?*
> *I've travel't Skiddaw roond an' roond;*
> *An' theer war hunters than:*
> *Bit I was gayly oft wi' t'furst,*
> *An' went whoar nobbut odduns durst,*
> *An' nin noo leeven can.*

Looking north through the Vale of St John to Saddleback (Blencathra)

An' than at fair or merry-neet,
Nin like me cud ha' us't their feet;
　　An' theer war dancers than:
What! noo they fidge and run aboot
Theer nowder jig, three reel, nor nowt,
　　An' steps they hevvent yan.

When I was young, lads us't to larn
To dance, an' run, an' russel, barn,
　　'Twas few 'at larn't to read:
Fwok thowt their barns war sharp an' reet,
If they cud use their hands an' feet;
　　'Twas laal they car't for t'heid.

Fwok use' to drink good heàmm brew't yal,
It steud on t'teàble ivvery meàll,
　　An' ye mud swig yr're fill:
Bit noo theer nowt bit swashy tea,
Na wonder fwok sud warsent be,
　　Fair snafflins they'll be still

This warld an' me are beàth alike,
We're beàth on t'shady side o' t'dyke,
　　An' tumlen fast doon t'broo:
Theer nowt 'at nivver yan can see,
'At's hofe like what it use' to be;
　　Aw things ur feckless noo!

A bridleway below the church runs straight down into the heart of the vale. This route provides an attractive and varied walk. Directly across the valley are the quarry levels, great scars gouged out of the inhospitable fellside. Even when the sunlight pours into them, they make a startling contrast to the quiet green fields that stretch towards the massive bulk of Blencathra. Our path runs immediately above the fell wall. Autumn is the best season in a place like this, when the bracken on the stony slopes above is dying back in a confusion of russet and gold. It is an unfrequented way, so peaceful that a person can hear the acorns falling from the mature oaks lined along the lower side of the wall. There are fence posts placed against the stones on our side, topped with netting, to deter the sheep from scrambling over.

St John's Beck is flowing gently along the valley bottom today, but the embankments lining its course are a reminder of the fearful storms of rain that are a regular feature of life in the Lakeland dales. Occasionally the downpours are so catastrophic that the record of them passes into history. Mannex' *Cumberland Directory* of 1847, for example, describes the events of August 22, 1749, in the Vale of St John: *There fell here such a waterspout as in less than two hours deluged the whole valley many feet deep, sweeping away all the bridges* (each farm on the west side of the valley still has its own bridge), *walls, houses etc., and so effectively erasing the corn mill that one of its stones has not been found to this day. A short distance from where the mill stood, an excavation was made in the side of the mountain that*

Ancient crossing place of St John's Beck near Bridge End Farm; stepping stones and packhorse bridge

would hold St. Paul's. This remarkable fall of water was accompanied with the most terrible thunder and incessant lightning imaginable...

A similar cataclysm had overwhelmed the Hawkshead area on the night of June 10, 1686, so memorable as to have been enshrined in the parish register, when: *there was such a fearfull thunder with fyre and rayne, which occasioned such a terrible flood, as the like of it was never seene in these parts of no man liveinge, for it did throwe down some houses and mills, and tooke away severall briggs...* And Mrs Linton tells how on September 9, 1760, a waterspout had burst on Grasmoor during one of these tremendous storms, and devastated with stones ten acres, which *no human art can ever restore.*

These have been the exceptional occurrences, and normally the shepherd or the forester accepts the rain as just another fact of life. There are probably more words for different degrees of wetness in the Lake District than in any other part of the country. Mrs Linton quotes Harriet Martineau's report of a dalesman's description of weather out on the fells: *It donks and dozzles, and whiles it's a bit siftering, but it don't often make no girt pell.* Nevertheless, the current ten-year average rainfall in Coniston exceeds 100 inches, and in the last eighty years the annual total has fallen below seventy inches only once - 67.82 in 1933 (statistics courtesy of Mr J.W.B.Hext, from the records kept at Holywath, Coniston).

However, any "girt pell" on this particular autumn morning seems most unlikely; cloud is now clearing from Blencathra summit, and the lower slopes are serenely sunlit in contrast to the deep shadows above. Its white houses, apparently set among trees, make Threlkeld look quite picturesque from this enchanted distance. But no amount of sunlight could ever make the rugged crags on the eastern side of the vale appear anything but formidable. Their presence casts its own shadow - they are so barren, and the untidy, shapeless areas of scree run down greedily almost to the road. It is pleasanter to look towards the head of the valley. The low fells beneath which we are walking are of the more usual Lake District knobbly type. They curve round gradually, almost to meet the eastern crags against the famous Castle Rock. The Jaws of Borrowdale spring to mind - this could easily be the head of the valley, beyond which the uninhabitable wilderness takes over.

Meanwhile, we can enjoy the immediate Arcadian surroundings as the vale narrows before us. Some small plantations give a kindlier appearance than the unbroken bracken cover; as the track drops right to the valley floor, the remains of the summer flower carpet are still striking, even in September - a scatter of harebells, quantities of yarrow, shining stars of tormentil and little clumps of chickweed. Our bridleway must once have been of much greater significance as a route than it is today. On the upper side is the wreck of an old wall; on the lower, a substantial field dyke. The oaks that lined the way below the church have given way to ash trees that were once pollarded regularly, to make poles and to provide nibbling for the sheep. One, hollow with age, has been blown over, but some of its roots still cling to the soil, and delicate white poles rise from its head at right angles to the gnarled and mossy trunk.

Approaching the farm at Low Bridge End, the bridleway has turned into a narrow path. The amount of noise that the sheep are making suggests that they have only recently been separated from the main flock, and put into an unfamiliar pasture. Every few yards, a neat flat stone on the pathway marks the line of a little drainage sike. Some of these sikes have created miniature moss-covered gorges, where the bonsai-size trees and ferns that grow alongside make them into natural rock gardens. Then, beyond the farm, the valley

Windermere. Steamers at rest

Sunset over the Leven estuary

Reflections, Thirlmere

really does taper away to nothing. The river and the road run below crags on either side; the dark outline of Blencathra completely shuts off the view behind. There is space only for a single field, flecked with sheep and closed in by the big trees that shelter the farm buildings. Yet suddenly, over the bend in the river, it all begins to open out once more. Green fields are visible through the trees ahead, the sky becomes wider, and somehow, brighter; as we pick our way over the tree roots by the margin of the swiftly flowing river, Isaac Watts' lines come to mind:

Sweet fields beyond the swelling flood
Stand dressed in living green...

But before we can get to this promised land, we have to climb high above the stream along a narrow footway. Tree branches, or whole carcasses of trees lie spread-eagled on the scree - ready-made sculptures that have fallen from their precarious roothold on the rockface. Soon we find ourselves in a patch of old woodland - mainly oak, with a mixture of birch, rowan and ash. This is much more the conventional 'beautiful Lake District' than most of St John's Vale, but the individuality remains. The drop to the river is precipitous, and there is an unexpected tang in the air, vaguely recalling the smell of new pencils. The explanation comes quickly enough, when we notice the wood yard on the other side.

At this point, we have reached the area where the Vale of St John merges into the long narrow valley which Thirlmere now fills and which, after more than a century, has not acquired a generally acknowledged dale-name. As we emerge from the oak wood we look up to the sombre western flank of Helvellyn; across the busy road below us is Bridge End Farm. Great How behind the farm closes the way to Thirlmere as effectively as Castle Crag seals off upper Borrowdale from Grange. We must either take the main road through the gap ahead, or follow the river and go by the west of Great How to Thirlmere dam.

Thirlspot, in the middle of the eastern gap, is one of the popular jumping-off points for the Helvellyn plod. There is even a line of whitened stones to mark the way. This uninviting fell land barely stops short at the buildings of the inn, leaving only one field's width of reasonable land between the fell wall and the road. (One of these fields sports a set of football goalposts, but during the week is likely to be thronged with sheep.) It is not surprising, therefore, that the profusion of natural stone has created many strange forms; more surprising is to come across a watercourse running the 'wrong' way. This part of the Thirlmere gathering system traps the streams in mid-flow, and diverts the water back into the reservoir. To reach the head of the dale from here it is not necessary to go down to the road, because there are paths through the forest all the way to Wythburn, where the church is all that remains of the little dales community that was drowned in 1890. The hamlet was always known as the city - not, one feels sure, in any sarcastic sense. Almost certainly the word is really the Scandinavian 'saetr', found in place names such as Satterthwaite or Ambleside, and meaning a summer pasture.

The church is very small; and dark inside. According to Baddeley, it was perhaps the smallest in England before the chancel was added in 1872, and also one of the most old-fashioned. He relates how, by the side of the old pulpit, was a narrow slit, or 'grike' as it would be known locally, into which, on one occasion, the preacher had the misfortune to drop his sermon notes as he was preparing to begin his address. Finding all his efforts to recover it futile, he turned to his congregation and, taking up the Bible, remarked: "Brethren, I've dropped t'sermon doon t'grike, but I'll read a chapter in t'Bible that's

Thirlmere and Raven Crag

worth twal' of it."

We may be certain that this possibly apocryphal story pre-dated the ministry of the Rev Basil Lawson, who served here from 1849 to 1892. During his earliest years in the valley he kept a diary, which brings the older community vividly to life. He noted the comings and goings of the tourists with particular detail if they were proposing to climb Helvellyn. One of the tracks to the summit takes off from the road near to the church, and some of these visitors figure in the diary as failures - a condition they share with the writer, who has been turned back by adverse weather conditions each time he has set out for the top! In Lawson's time Wythburn was a popular halt for coaches. There was the Nag's Head opposite the church, where visitors could fortify themselves before the climb or recuperate afterwards; and, a little way to the north, the Cherry Tree, which figures in Wordsworth's poem *The Waggoner.*

Lawson took an equal interest in the local people, and jotted down the events that made up the cycle of the farmer's year - sowing of oats in the front field, or John Gillbanks washing his sheep, clipping them, or carrying grain. He was himself a keen follower of the Blencathra pack, and noted when John Crozier brought his hounds to the neighbourhood of the city. He would follow them on foot, as did everyone else. A horse was, and is, of no use in Lakeland fox-hunting, which does not remotely resemble the hunting of the Shires, so graphically described in Lawson's own lifetime by Surtees or Trollope.

The huntsman and his small band of foot followers cast about in the higher intakes, or on the open ground above the fell wall, hoping to find the drag - the scent leading from wherever the fox has been that night to the place where he is lying up. Once a fox is scented and found, the outcome rests between him and the hounds. There is very little the huntsman can do to influence the course of events once a chase has begun. They may lose the scent and circle vainly over the fellside; two or three hounds may go off on a tack of their own and be returned the next day by a friendly farmer from the next valley; an energetic and observant follower may glimpse the fox from a vantage point some distance from the toiling hounds, and bring them up sharp with a stentorian "Halloo". There is no telling whether a fox will be put up - no helpful keepers to draw coverts - no certain way of knowing which direction he will take, or even whether the scenting will be good. The only certainty is that a considerable element of luck will be needed to catch the fox.

Basil Lawson then, a century and more ago, striding across the scree, stick in hand, wearing stout boots and a thick jacket, would be indistinguishable from the farmers and shepherds whose henrun or flock had been worried. He was perhaps more observant, because he always kept an eye open for anything of interest in the natural world, or for a scene which he could later recreate with pencil or watercolours. His walks over the fells were not confined to hunting days, either. Visiting his parishioners must have involved a lot of strenuous legwork, rewarded not only by welcome cups of tea on his arrival, but also by the strengthening of those bonds which linked the members of his scattered flock together.

Today there is no community in this upper portion of the valley, and an unending stream of traffic moves along the road below the church. But the pedestrian may still experience a sense of place by taking the minor road on the west side of the reservoir. Right at the start we have the opportunity to appreciate the majestic scale of the dam by which the reservoir was created. Then, walking above the shore, through the mainly coniferous

Waterfalls, Raise Beck

plantations, we are in an almost alpine ambience, unique in the Lakeland dales. The best time to capture this atmosphere is on a calm day, when the level of the lake is high, and the reflections of the dark trees clinging to the craggy slopes go some way towards compensating for the world that has been lost. Finally, emerging from the plantation towards Armboth, we are back in a familiar dale-head, noisy streams tumbling from the crowding fells, a straggle of sheep newly released from the pens above the road broadcasting strong whiffs of disinfectant over the still air, and two or three young folk striding away beneath their rucksacks. In order to reach our next valley, we should follow their example, if possible, by taking the mountain path over Fairfield into Dovedale, en route for Patterdale.

Kirk Stone, Kirkstone Pass

X: Patterdale and Ullswater

*All about Ullswater, on both sides, are multitudes of glens that run up behind the
mountains, and thread them like garden paths about their feet.*

Mrs Linton.

CROSSING one of the highest mountains barriers in England is not an easy option, but
the reward of climbing up from Wythburn is that it is possible to descend into Dovedale.
The vale of Ullswater is distinguished by the way in which several tributary valleys run into
it from the Helvellyn massif, and Dovedale is the one nearest to Kirkstone foot. The scene
here has changed little since Wordsworth's day. It is still *seldom visited by travellers* and is
still *richly decorated with native wood*. Indeed, the combination of green pastures on the
valley floor with groups of mature trees gives it the air of a slightly neglected parkland.
Everything is so calm and quiet, the only movement the swish of a tail as one of the black
cattle standing together in the shade idly flicks away the flies.

Deepdale, running into the main valley below Brothers Water is bigger, sparser and
longer than Dovedale: there, the trees thin gradually until the high vertical crags prohibit
any kind of anchorage; here, the green changes abruptly to brown beyond the fell wall. The
bridge, just three huge stone slabs, with a watery chaos of boulders on both sides, sets the
tone of stark and rather melancholy grandeur. It really is a deep dale, hemmed in by stern,
forbidding mountains, terminated, to quote Wordsworth again: *by a cove, a craggy and
gloomy abyss, with precipitous sides; a faithful receptacle of the snows that are driven into it, by*

the West wind, from the summit of Fairfield.

Grisedale, which runs up from the very head of Ullswater, is bigger still, and in its lower reaches almost as romantically picturesque as Dovedale. But it is much more frequented, by reason of the well-trodden paths to the hause at its head and directly to Helvellyn summit. First, there is a steep climb with the stream far below in a deep wooded ravine. Then, on more level and fertile ground, Braesteads and Elm How form a microcosm of the traditional dales landscape. The green fields are an oasis by comparison with the encroaching wilderness; the sheltering trees provide protection from the rain and wind that sweep so fiercely down; yet at the same moment (Wordsworth again): *a sublime combination of mountain forms appears in front while ascending the bed of this valley.* The higher we ascend, the rougher the going becomes. On an autumn morning the rays of sunlight fan out from the ridge of St Sunday Crag; the only company has been the busy little sheep with black faces and small horns. Suddenly one of them appears on top of the wall ahead, and steps delicately down like a cat.

As the sun moves round, we step out of the shadow to begin the steep pull up to the hause. A solitary climber is spreadeagled against the face of one of the lower crags; the buttresses along the top of St Sunday Crag are no longer in shadow and alternate with the dark gullies that divide them. Fairfield and Dollywagon Pike close the valley ahead: looking back, Place Fell, flooded by the mid-day sunlight, reminds us that our subject is Ullswater.

The fourth tributary valley is the best known, and runs straight up from Glenridding village. The houses soon peter out, then the tree-lined way forks - left to Lanty Tarn, on the way either to Helvellyn or down again into Grisedale, and right to Greenside. Bleak, angular scree spills from the base of the crags along the top of the mountain wall. The atmosphere as we climb farther into the glen recalls that of the Coppermines Valley above Coniston - not surprising perhaps, considering that this was also an important mining area. Most people press on through Glenridding, eager to attain the heights and certainly there is less to detain the *Artist or leisurely Traveller* (Worsdworth) than in either Grisedale or Glencoyne, a short distance farther again along the shore of Ullswater. This last and relatively little valley is quieter, more sylvan, recalling Dovedale, where we began. It is characteristic that the group of miners' cottages near one of the secondary entrances to the mines is known (even marked on the map) as 'Seldom Seen'.

Glencoyne is a tiny kingdom in itself: there is Glencoyne Wood, Glencoyne Farm (one of the National Trust's premier sheep farms) and Glencoyne Park. Here is Lyulph's Tower, built in a self-consciously 'picturesque', pseudo-mediaeval style and, in fact, an early nineteenth century shooting lodge constructed for the Duke of Norfolk. Glencoyne Wood, Aira Beck Woods and Gowbarrow Park all belong to the National Trust, so the whole area is well managed, and waymarked. Even a timid walker can totter up to Aira Force, where the falls, after heavy rain, are as dramatic, not to say breathtaking, as the guidebooks make them out to be. But none of these valleys should intimidate the average or the unadventurous pedestrian. Mrs Linton was decidedly tart on this point: *As independent walks,* she observed, *they are within the compass of any south country woman who can walk beyond her own garden.*

Different as each valley has been in character and appearance, a common thread links them, the mines. They are here, even in Arcadian Dovedale. A channel, cut from Dovedale Beck as it leaps and tumbles down the fellside, connects with a small holding reservoir

Hartsop Hall

from which a water leat runs for about a mile round the fell breast to the extensive remains of mine workings quarter of a mile west of Hartsop Hall. This very old lead mine was not abandoned until 1942, and then not because the vein had been exhausted. W.T.Shaw and his father, who had been working the mine since 1931, dismantled and removed all the plant, so that now the area is completely desolate.

The ruins of the buildings which had housed the crusher and smelter stand amid the spoil heaps. Nearby are the old entrance passages to the mines - adits - the horizontal tunnels leading to the ore veins. One is situated just behind the rough platform above the highest spoil heap. It is possible to see where the waste was barrowed along before being tipped over the edge. The native trees are now beginning to colonise the tips, giving the blackness of the adits a particularly sinister appearance by contrast. At the watery entrance to one of them, just high enough for a smallish man to go in without stooping, the morning sun shines directly on the vivid green ferns that form a partial veil over the mouth. Wafts of cold air drift across your face: from somewhere inside comes the sound of water dripping. As you shudder to think of the men who had to spend their working lives in these terrible holes, the sardonic cry of a woodpecker rings out from the trees below.

This is Hartsop Hall Mine; the Eagle Crag Mine in Grisedale is in a more open situation. Here too, although there has been no mining for over a century, is a long, narrow vein that has never been tackled. There were seven levels in all, and the remains of the workings lie some way below Ruthwaite Lodge. It should be remembered that most of the old mines were very small-scale affairs, not necessarily worked continuously. Three or four men would gain a modest livelihood from driving a level into the rock, and doing everything themselves - building their own smithy and powder house, sorting the ore, and operating the hand-washing floors.

The really big enterprise, comparable in scale with the Coniston copper mines, was the Greenside Mine high above Glenridding village, which did not close until 1962. Baddeley did not mince his words when he contemplated its environmental impact: *The Greenside Smelting Mills, a group of buildings whose hideousness we would rather not dwell upon. Suffice it to say that they mar hopelessly what was once a very beautiful valley.* Now the mines have become a magnet for industrial archaeologists and, as the memory of what working conditions were like begins to fade, they are acquiring a sort of romantic aura. One who worked there in the 1930s, cutting sleepers at the sawmill, recalls how he would walk on the tram rail for a mile or so into the mine. There was an electric bogie which pulled the trucks, powered by two wires overhead and protected only by a series of wooden boards. The end of each shift was marked for the joiner working outside by the lights on the miners' caps flashing and bobbing as their clogs clinked very fast along the line. Old people in Coniston remember the sound of those days, too: clogs plodding uphill early in the morning and clattering helter-skelter down in the evening.

The miners have made a place for themselves in the folk memory of Patterdale and Coniston, which will become part of the Lake District mythology like the quarrymen dicing with death each time they brought a loaded sledge down from Honister. James Clarke (in his *Survey of the Lakes*, 1789) wrung his hands over the social impact of the mines. Once, Patterdale had been as near as it is possible to get to an earthly paradise. Now: *the scene is changed. Vice and poverty sit pictured in almost every countenance.* The reason? The miners. *These fellows, who are in general the most abandoned, wicked and profligate part of mankind,*

Dovedale

no sooner settled here than they immediately began to propagate their vices among the innocent unsuspecting inhabitants. Two generations later Mrs Linton was less disposed to be censorious, perhaps because she took advantage of the opportunity to go into Coniston copper mines to see for herself. Not so desolate-looking, she felt, as the Greenside Mines, and with *a more heartsome and inhabited appearance generally.* It wasn't the miners who intrigued her, so much as the other denizens - not the 'knockers', for whom the miners used to leave suitable bits from their bait boxes, but the rats which added credibility to the presence of the knockers by eating up all these offerings.

The alternative way to approach Patterdale from Thirlmere is to follow the motor road all the way to Ambleside, then back to the top of Kirkstone Pass up the 'Struggle', most aptly named in the days when most transport was horse-drawn. It is not always possible to look down Patterdale from here, but the mysterious grandeur of the scene is then compensation enough, especially on a day of low, shifting cloud, and fine, drizzly rain. Wordsworth was here on just such a day in November 1805 and later, in his *Journal*, summed up his reaction with a masterly understatement: *This situation, it must be allowed, is not favourable to gaiety.* James Clarke, fortunately, had a clearer day when he was making his cartographic survey. He noted *rock upon rock, precipice above precipice, some fixed, others like to tumble down on each side of you.*

That sort of feeling can still take hold of a person up there, and not dissolve until the relative tranquillity of Brothers Water is reached. This lake was originally Broad Water, a much more appropriate descriptive name, as it almost fills the width of the valley between Dovedale and Hartsop. For the walker, the path by Hartsop Hall along the western shore of the lake is the one to follow. The hall, like that at Coniston, is now a bigger-than-average farmhouse, but has clearly been a place of consequence in days gone by. The pastoral charm of Brothers Water matches Dovedale, a welcome antidote to the wild mountains that press in on every side.

Hartsop village lies at the foot of yet another valley that cuts into the mountains, but on the east side of the dale. It is an old settlement of stone cottages, set higgledy-piggledy in all sorts of improbable relationships with each other. A few have the so-called 'spinning galleries' outside the upper floor: several have been 'modernised', but not garishly. Little walled footways run from place to place or down to the river. Weavers and miners made up the bulk of the population for generations. The sheep that sustained the one are still here, nibbling at the bumpy fields beyond the village, but the miners have left no more than a memory and the remains of their workings at the confluence of Hayeswater Gill and Pasture Beck.

This mine, Myers Head, met its end in circumstances more fitted to the heroic legends of the 'old men' than a mundane closure dictated by economic pressure. Water had always been a problem. A great wheel turned night and day to operate a pump which struggled to cope with the water draining into the mine. Then, one day in 1877, the miners unexpectedly broke into a large cavity in the vein. W.T.Shaw, in his *Mining in the Lake Counties*, relates how a kind of Wagnerian Götterdämmerung ensued. The flood of water pursued the fleeing miners as they struggled to safety up the ladders, bits and pieces of their tackle floating inches below the feet of the last man up.

From Hartsop a bridleway runs the whole distance to the head of Ullswater. In springtime the air is brighter than in the autumn, but more heavily laden. Bluebells

Remains of watermill race, Hayeswater Gill, Patterdale

sprinkle the wayside; all the way from Kirkstone the hawthorns on the fellside have been in full bloom. You always feel that the valley you happen to be in at that moment must be the loveliest of them all; James Clarke's equation of Patterdale with paradise becomes credible, and receives startling confirmation from two enormous wheelibins at Hartsop Fold road end - each is clearly labelled 'EDEN'. From over here it is obvious how Deepdale is no more than a cleft in the high mountain line. The nearer slopes are more sympathetic, where the native trees form a cover of varied green.

We continue past Beckstones, one of the many farms so named in the Lake District, and Crookabeck, and on to Rooking which, like Hartsop, has moved up the social scale. Old houses modernised, conversions and new building mix with a pleasing informality, the harshness of their stone tempered by the large and lavishly planted gardens which surround them. Yet none is more delightful than the flowery hay meadow over the road, quiet foreground to Grisedale and the Helvellyn ridge, deeply scarred by the tracks leading to the summit. A little farther along, and our way forks, at Side Farm. It would be possible to carry straight on to Sandwick and then Howtown, but that would mean missing Patterdale and Glenridding completely.

Patterdale has all the fixtures of a living village, including hall, school, pubs and recreation ground laid out for cricket as well as football. Glenridding has become more the focus for casual visitors - a vast car park, numerous eateries and postcard shops. Rowing boats are pulled up on the shingle by the cheerful little bay; one of the lake 'steamers', as they are still known, lies at the pier built where flood debris was deposited in 1927 after the dam burst above the mines, releasing the contents of the reservoir which held the head of water needed to supply power for the mine machinery.

In between the two villages, conveniently close to Patterdale Hall is Saint Patrick's Church, though his well is in the village, just beyond the cenotaph. Most people who visit the church, however, are less interested in the saint than in the extraordinarily gifted craftswoman who made her home in the valley - Ann Macbeth. It was in 1921 that she came to live permanently in Patterdale, where she was to stay until her death in 1948. After training at the Glasgow School of Art, she had already become known nationally for her work in needlecraft and ceramics. She was as energetic as she was gifted, and within a very short time had helped to found the Patterdale Women's Institute. She painted and fired pottery and china, painted in watercolours, designed stained glass windows, altar frontals and banners that were exhibited throughout Europe, and held classes in Patterdale for ladies interested in embroidery and handicraft.

Miss Macbeth soon became a familiar figure, tall and slim, unmistakable in her brightly coloured, slightly eccentric clothes, always accompanied by her little dog. Distinguished and famous though she was, she was also able to relate easily to her neighbours, sharing a laugh and ready to lend a helping hand in adversity. Many stories came to be told of her thoughtfulness and imaginative generosity - some local families still possess pottery pieces that she had painted and given to mark a family celebration, a christening, perhaps, or a silver wedding. It is said that when her own infant nephew won first prize in a local baby show, she painted a plate for each child who had been a competitor.

But it is in Saint Patrick's Church that her public memorial remains. Hanging inside are several examples of her work. The best known is 'The Good Shepherd', executed in

Exercising the trail hounds, Hartsop, Patterdale

wool and silk, in which Christ is depicted against precisely the background of fells to be seen from Wordsworth Cottage, Rooking, where Miss Macbeth lived when she was working on this piece. Greens and blues dominate what is clearly a springtime colour scheme, emphasised not just by the presence of two not wholly convincing lambs, but also by the wonderful parade of blooms dancing right across the foreground - hazel catkins, daisies, daffodils, primroses, bluebells, blackthorn and clover. Underpinning all, below the frame of the picture, are the first bars of Parry's music for *Jerusalem!* Members of the W.I. never fail to break into song at the sight of this panel. The large companion piece, 'The Nativity', belongs to Glasgow Corporation, but is exhibited regularly at Patterdale. Then, farther along the south wall of the church is a smaller panel showing a bowl of flowers, a tour de force in the art of painting with a needle.

The work which has the closest emotional involvement with the life of the valley hangs just beside the door. It is a panel (approximately 90cm x 75cm) consisting of five roundels, worked in dark colours, mainly russet, brown and grey, so that the dove in the central one stands out vividly as she descends on the mountain-girt lake - unmistakably Ullswater. Then the four subsidiary roundels show us the life that goes on beneath that blessing: a farmer surrounded by his sheep, and holding a tiny lamb; the farmer's wife feeding her poultry in the yard; the village children walking to school; an old man with his dog by the fireside of his cottage. The inscription above and below the roundels reads:

Christ keep the mountain lands all winter through,
And bless the farm, and bless the school, and bless the fireside too.

Everything in these scenes is absolutely authentic. The local detail is superb - for example, the kitchen range in the old cottage, the covers on the table and the back of the chair are exactly what the artist must have seen as she perhaps called to bring that old man his newspaper on a wet, cold January day. Finally, on the west side of the door is a fine oblong panel, of two birds facing each other in the midst of thick fruiting foliage. The colours here are mainly greens, with browns and grey again. Ann Macbeth's range is wonderfully demonstrated by the contrast of this generalised, almost abstract piece to the homely particulars across the way. The dignified inscription serves to emphasise the point - we are not now addressing John, the local farmer, but Everyman:

Peace when Thou comest and when Thou goest;
May Thy footsteps echo Peace.

With this benediction to help us on our way, we return to Side Farm, crossing the strath at the head of the lake. There is more than a hint of the Scottish Highlands as we continue under the lee of Place Fell, in the direction of Howtown. From here it is possible to see how Ullswater begins as an almost land-locked, cosy little basin, an ideal recreation area for those who hire rowing boats. Soon the juniper which for a time has dominated the ground cover on the fellside gives way to birch. Some of the trees are old and gnarled, but small seedlings are scattered among the dark, angular rocks below the path. It may be the birches that give the Scottish flavour; that, and the geology. The rock here is darker than in much of the Lake District, and the lake, in its upper reaches, surprisingly narrow, crowded and constrained by its attendant mountains.

The path takes a switchback course, now down at lake level, next way above, giving the opportunity to see those tributary valleys on the other side. Glencoyne looks particularly attractive, with its combination of fields and copses. Somewhere among the

Ullswater from the Howtown path

trees a hunt is in progress; hounds are giving mouth, and the unmusical blare of the huntsman's horn echoes across the water. In the days when the Lakes were first 'discovered' some imaginative entrepreneur hit on the idea of exploiting the echo potential and, with the aid of a French horn from somewhere near Watermillock, would create a noise like that "of a great orchestra" reverberating round the fells. What the Duke of Norfolk and his friends in their 'picturesque' hunting retreat thought, is not recorded, but they were all taking part in the same charade.

The only habitation between Side Farm and Howtown is at Sandwick, still a wonderfully quiet little spot, needing no echo effects or Gothic trimmings to create an atmosphere. By now, the woodland is more mixed - predominantly oak, but with beech and alder as well as birch. Before dropping to Howtown we may pause to look, not at the mountains now, but at the lower reaches of the lake, too lightly dismissed by Baddeley as "tame". *Lady of the Lake* is chugging into Howtown bay, bringing another cargo of fortunate holidaymakers who are about to walk these paths. Apart from her, there is very little activity on the blue sunlit water; only one or two more adventurous yachtsmen, who have perhaps come up from Pooley Bridge. The headland opposite, approximately dividing mountain Ullswater from pastoral Ullswater is Skelly Nab, reminding us by its name of a feature of this lake that is now largely forgotten. Just as Coniston has its char, Ullswater has its skellies, or schellies. When he came this way in November 1805, Wordsworth was fortunate enough to see three fishermen drawing their nets ashore, *and hundreds of fish were leaping in their prison.* He goes on: *They were all of the kind called skellies, a sort of fresh-water herring, shoals of which may sometimes be seen dimpling or rippling the surface of the lake in calm weather. This species is not found, I believe in any other of these lakes.*

Howtown itself is no bigger than Sandwick, but is the calling place for the steamers, and the end of the road up from Pooley Bridge past Sharrow Bay. There is a lot of coming and going along the carefully laid path from the boat landing, but not a lot of other activity. The liveliest feature is the ducks which come winging in with the boats, no doubt hoping to pick up a free lunch from the visitors' sandwich packs. The black cattle in the level field in front of the farm do not even turn their heads to see who is passing. Howtown to Pooley Bridge is a pleasant stroll for anyone with physical or emotional energy left after coming all the way from Brothers Water. A very satisfying alternative is to take the steamer, either from here, or all the way from Glenridding. This is perhaps the best of all the Lakeland sails. Every feature of the majestic scene is as clear as from the path, especially since the course runs close to the wilder eastern shore. And then the lower reach, the mountains no more than a distant memory, is like some great river, as we glide imperceptibly out of the Lake District into more ordinary, albeit charming, rural landscape.

Haweswater dam

XI: Haweswater and Kentmere

It is a grand walk all along the edge of Haweswater, under the eaves of the mountain ridges, with that great Wallow Crag on your flank, and Harter Fell and the other rough Mardale mountains before you.

Mrs Linton.

FROM POOLEY Bridge through Askham and Bampton to Burnbank underneath Haweswater dam, we cross the kind of green pastoral landscape which is characteristic of so much of the Lakeland fringe. As with the western dales, the transition to 'the Lake District' is abrupt. The mountains begin to take over as we approach Burnbank. This somewhat forlorn settlement has an unusual appearance, because it consists largely of houses, some unoccupied, left over, as it were from the time when the lake was turned into a reservoir. It is a suitably sad memorial to the rape of a lovely valley. Only the grand scale of the dominating mountain lines remains unaltered.

From Burnbank the pedestrian may continue on either side of the water. Each has its own advantages. The track along the western shore is not accessible to the car-borne visitors who home in whenever there has been a drought to see the ruins of the old village at the head of the dale. Usually, however, the metalled road on the east is quiet enough. The steep hillside above is dark and rocky. Ferns and old trees cling as best they can - either there has been a decline since Baddeley came in pre-reservoir days, or he allowed his imagination to run ahead a little; *craggy, precipitous and richly draped with forest foliage*, he wrote of Wallow Crag.

Soon we come to the Haweswater Hotel, which looks rather as if it should be adjoining a railway station. It was built as part of the reservoir project, to replace the famed Dun Bull, drowned at the inundation. Without doubt the standards of accommodation and service there are far superior to anything the old inn could ever provide, but it suffers from an impossible psychological handicap as the romantic aura of the past thickens with the passing of time. The lake itself, like Thirlmere, has a very real disadvantage - the ugly draw-down scar which has replaced the natural shore, a stony line scored across the landscape between the water and the bare fellsides. Beyond the hotel, the open deciduous woodland above the road thins away to nothing as the prospect becomes still wilder. The mountains ahead, on a November morning, are a dark silhouette against the midday sun. On the other side of the lake, a silent valley runs obliquely up to a sombre corrie below the looming bulk of Whelter Crags.

Our road is now high above the lake, giving a fine panoramic view over the dale. The old walls on the far side have not disintegrated. They run meaninglessly through the dead bracken, across the draw-down scar, and vanish into the water. There is an area of flatter ground at the foot of Riggindale, through which one of the principal feeder streams of the reservoir runs. Here, every drought reveals the drowned field pattern below the Rigg. This is a humpy peninsula, presently covered by conifers, which almost cuts off the upper reach of the lake, where the valley has narrowed into a sunless cleft reaching into the heart of the mountains. Riggindale runs at right angles to the lake, the corrie at its head cut in half by deep shadow. Kidsty Pike, a really pointed mountain summit from this position, brings the dale to a dramatic climax. In fact, this landscape parallels that above Patterdale; the High Street range, like Helvellyn, presents its rugged and exciting face to the east.

Not that our own side of the lake is lacking in drama. The stones and debris that litter the road are a reminder of the force with which the becks can sweep down the mountainside. It is worth taking the track which leads from this point opposite Riggindale eventually over to Swindale, the old 'corpse road'. The ascent, past two small disused quarries, is so steep that a kestrel hanging in the air nearer to the lake, is at eye-level. A considerable flotilla of geese who have been minding their own business just off-shore suddenly takes off in the direction of the Rigg in a flurry of white foam and confused honking. Its movement draws attention to the field pattern which has now become clear by the outfall of the beck below. What was once a huddle of tiny paddocks, recalling Wasdale Head, is now a maze of walls enclosing only stones. The corpse road, well constructed and embanked on its lower side, curves away from the gill above the point at which the stream forks and retreats into two fearsome, dark ravines.

Winding up and on, the road cuts through the rock where necessary, and the coffin bearers were able to rest at the edge of the high wide moor dividing Mardale from Swindale. Haweswater is far below us now, but we are still within the orbit of what was once the life of Mardale. There are several ruinous buildings up here - summer bothies for shepherds or herdsmen, hoghouses to shelter sheep or stock, maybe peat scales like the ones above Boot in Eskdale for storing fuel - but whatever their purpose, obviously an essential element in the seasonal round for folk toiling up this road generation after generation.

The gill which has marked the line of the corpse road tumbles into the lake over gigantic boulders. It is not far from here to the end of the metalled road. Below the small

Haweswater and old Mardale

car park, grass has begun to grow again on fields submerged only in times of flood; the two straight walls between which the road ran out of the village look perfectly serviceable. Very soon this old cart road turns into a bridle path just beyond the car park. It is easy to see why Haweswater was so attractive to reservoir engineers. Three sizable streams converge: one from Blea Water below High Street; one from Gatescarth, by which pass a person may cross into Longsleddale; and one, which we shall follow, from Nan Bield, that separates Mardale from the Kentmere valley. The place is loud with the sound of waterfalls, tracing irregular and ever-changing white foaming lines across the brown hillsides. Our track goes up under Piot Crag, which curves round to join the huge forbidding vertical face of High Street, now spectacularly illuminated by the horizontal rays of the winter sun. On our left, the lower slopes of Harter Fell soon turn into inaccessible crags where a raven croaks. The fell walls, marking the utmost limits of the intakes for rough pasture, swoop up and down the stony wilderness ahead. There is no-one else on the bridleway; back by the reservoir, the few visitors in the car park sit in their vehicles, pecking at sandwiches.

We are in one of the most impenetrable parts of the Lake District, and maybe one of the benefits of the reservoir has been to make human access even more difficult. The seasoned fell walker and the golden eagle share these lonely uplands. They seem to get on well enough without the Dun Bull, and before we cross into Kentmere, a final look back with an abrasive counterblast to romantic idealising of the past - from Mrs Linton: *In truth, it is all very primitive and rough; and it is easy to understand how fine gentlemen and ladies who travel with 'comforts', would shrink from the only place of entertainment at Haweswater as they would shrink from an Indian's wigwam; and for some of the same reasons. Then, it is not very practicable for grandees in their carriages; for the high road is a mere walled-in path, where two carts, if they met, would have to make compliments to each other, and one must back into the nearest gate... The church is picturesque enough...but it is by no means a rustic cathedral; the royal hotel (ie. the Dun Bull) is a wretched wayside public house, where you can get eggs and bacon and nothing else - except the company of a tipsy parson lying in bed with his gin bottle by his side; and the King of Mardale - the great man of the place, the largest landed proprietor of the home blood, and in his time the best wrestler and the best sheep shearer of the dale - is a yeoman.*

From the Nan Bield pass we drop quickly down to Kentmere reservoir - in size and appearance more like a big tarn - right underneath the mountain face. The dam was constructed so that the flow of water along the River Kent to the mills at Staveley down the valley could be regulated. Now the reservoir has become integrated into the landscape. High Street blocks the head of the dale; Harter Fell is on our left, and on the right a series of precipitous mountainsides - Froswick and Ill Bell and the almost sheer Rainsborrow Crag. Quite suddenly, even as we look, long folds of white misty cloud roll in to hide their summits, spilling over to fill the high corries. We are still in sunlight, but a cold wind has sprung up, drifting the mist in opaque curtains across the crags of Ill Bell, and sending it swirling down to the dark bowl which holds the reservoir.

Not that the scene is much more homely below the dam. Here are the long level spoil heaps of the old Kentmere quarries. There are deep holes in the fells on both sides of the valley. On the eastern slope a steep zigzag trod makes for the highest level, where there is the housing for a ropeway to bring the slate down. This is a dark slate, almost silver-grey, some of it curiously marked, so that when cut and polished it looks rather like marble.

Old quarry track, Kentmere

Everything is abandoned now, but the theme of desolation carried over from Mardale soon gives way to a more cheerful prospect.

Admittedly, the highest farm is derelict; but somehow, the atmosphere is not forlorn. Round about there are traces of settlement from prehistoric times, and it is as if Tongue House were waiting for the next tenants to arrive. The stone booses to accommodate the beasts in the shippon are intact, along with the passageway at their head to enable the stockman to bring bundles of hay from the adjacent barn. Two springs feed the long stone trough out in the yard, where the gate into the field still works properly. The field wall above the farm swings confidently up to the line of crags and scree that marks the last outpost of Harter Fell, helped on its way by a pair of outsize boulders deposited by the last glacier, that have been skilfully incorporated into its structure.

We have now reached the upper part of the Kentmere valley. There are trees again, ash mainly, often pollarded, with some oak and birch; the fields are green; sheep are grazing. Farther down, out of sight, someone is making a tractor work very hard. A noisy crowd of rooks settles on the soft ground nearer the river. The mist has cleared from the tops as suddenly as it descended, and we are in sunshine again. If John Bunyan had known about Kentmere, he would surely have used it as the model for one of the pleasant places through which Christian passed on his pilgrimage. It is a quiet valley, broad enough not to seem hemmed in by its mountains, but rather protected by them; and, being open to the south, lets in the sunshine and soft breezes - as well as the rains from the Atlantic depressions which swell the beck into a dangerous river that periodically devastates Kendal, far downstream. All the farms in this upper section of the valley are situated on the higher ground above the flood line. They are all old, the house often attached to the barn, with outbuildings of all shapes and sizes. Some gable ends have a rough crow-step design, not commonly seen in the Lake District. Everything is stone-built, and slate-roofed. Some of the quarrymen who mined the 'metal' lived in the scatter of cottages at Green Quarter a little farther along the valley.

However, from the farm called Overend, a footpath crosses the valley floor and leads to Kentmere village without going round that way. In fact there is a spider's web of little old paths criss-crossing the fields, linking farm with farm. Once, everyone walked everywhere; now, for the most part, they are not needed and are used only by visiting walkers. The sound of a tree crashing makes us aware again of the tractor that we heard earlier. Someone is extracting timber from the knobbly lower slopes near Green Quarter, and manoeuvring his trailer backwards with extraordinary skill. Bright winter sunshine now fills the valley. Beside our path sheep stand, almost dreamily, chewing and looking into the sun as if enjoying the lazy warmth. Soon we cross the river by a wooden footbridge and reach the next farm by way of some broken pasture, where black cattle are grazing among the boulders and holly trees.

We could have come down from the reservoir on this western side of the valley, passing above Hartrigg Farm. The full circuit makes a delightful stroll, meriting the same accolade that Baddeley gave to the neighbourhood of Rosthwaite in Borrowdale - only today, it is even quieter, except that several ducks, disturbed by our intrusion, explode out of the little stream below the road in the direction of the River Kent, upsetting the sheep by their loud quacking as they hurtle over the field. The comparison with Borrowdale is topographically apt also. Just as the Jaws above Grange divide the lower from the upper part of the valley,

Kentmere village from near Green Quarter

so the valley is pinched above Kentmere village, and the road takes a rocky leap past Heads to the magical world we are about to leave. Meanwhile, there is no incentive to hurry away.

From Kentmere churchyard we look beyond Kentmere Hall to the Garburn Pass, the ancient road connecting this valley with Troutbeck. The small irregular fields run up from the green pastures of the valley floor. The nearer to the open fell, the rougher the ground, and the larger the casual boulders which, presumably, a glacier left behind long ago. One is larger than the barn below us. At the foot of the pass, sharply picked out this morning by the sun, is the old hall. Like that at Coniston, it is mediaeval in origin, but extensively altered during the sixteenth century, when more modern living accommodation was added to the dour, defensive pele tower. Like Coniston, too, it was for long associated with a single family; in this case the Gilpins, who commanded the respect of the local community through many generations. A memorial tablet in Saint Cuthbert's Church gives one clue to the reasons for this respect. It concerns Bernard, and is inscribed:

> To the glory of God and in grateful memory of His servant Bernard Gilpin, born Kentmere Hall: of honourable lineage, he became fellow of Queens' and student of Christ Church Oxford… He accepted the principles of the Reformation and was one of its noble exponents in a perilous time. He faced the persecution of the Church and the anger of the queen, for truth and duty. A pattern parish priest, he was as saintly as he was brave, as generous as he was just, as practical as he was enthusiastic. An ardent student of scripture, he did not undervalue primitive tradition. An impassioned missionary, he won the name of the Apostle of the North, refusing all honours save the honour of serving his master, Christ. He kept a tender conscience, unspotted from the world, and left behind him an imperishable name. 1517-1588.

The Gilpin crest, on a scroll below this memorial, is surmounted by a boar, reminding us that this family had, at an earlier date, been renowned in another sphere of life. It was Richard who had first been given the lordship of Kentmere during the reign of King John *for his singular deserts in peace and war.* Tradition has it that he slew a particularly fierce wild boar which, raging in the mountains adjoining, had done much damage to the country people. On the south side of the churchyard is a big old yew tree, walled around just like the one at Torver, to make a circular stone seat. Looking down the valley from this seat, the river running quietly through the fields into a small lake roughly where Kent Mere used to be, wild boars are about the last thing to spring to mind.

The wildest creatures are some sheep, being gathered on the low hillside by a shepherd and two dogs. He is standing at one of the fell gates, and the dogs, partly responding to his calls, partly using their own assessment of the immediate situation, are bringing the flock together before escorting it down through the gate. Lakeland sheepdogs or, more properly, shepherds' dogs, are most commonly seen at work like this, but some of the shepherds find time to go along to the sheepdog trials that take place annually in many of the dales including Kentmere.

At a serious trials the atmosphere recalls that which used to prevail at county cricket matches. The spectators nearly all appreciate the finer points of the proceedings, and watch with a keen and knowledgeable interest. There is a kind of scoreboard on which the points

Kentmere Hall, Kentmere

awarded to each competitor are posted. (The judges will have been considering every aspect of the performance - the gathering, driving, penning, lifting, style, and so on.) After an innings is ended, the crowd applauds. This applause can vary from a polite ripple for the man who has made rather a hash of his opportunity, through a warmer round when someone has struggled well but unavailingly with an unusually bloody-minded set of sheep, to an enthusiastic clap for a polished, professional performance.

Meanwhile the shepherds awaiting their turn stand around trying to look unconcerned, like a man sitting outside the pavilion with his pads on, waiting for the next wicket to fall. "I think I'm on next," a young man in jeans and jersey is saying, trying his best to sound casual. Those who have been in can relax, with a drink and a crack amongst friends, but not before they have seen to the dog. One man returns from the arena, dog panting at his heel after a sterling effort that has put them in the lead and, opening the boot of his car, pours the dog a drink, saying: "Come on now, but you're not THAT good!" with an affectionate pat on the head.

No two rounds are alike, and the crowd will watch all day with the undiminished interest that a cricket aficionado can bestow on a whole string of maiden overs. For the more casual spectators (who are not numerous) the main interest comes when something unusual happens - the equivalent of a middle stump flying, or a six hit into the pavilion. Someone will get his three sheep to the pen as smoothly as can be, then they balk at going in; one presently enters, but the shepherd is now too eager. At the movement of his crook the others scatter, and the third one comes out again to see what is going on. Another brings his sheep straight down between the hurdles in the middle of the arena, then round the obstacle hurdles, and his dog, creeping slowly forward on his belly, nudges them into the pen before they know where they are. And we have scarcely heard a command or whistle all the time - a superb performance. But there is an element of luck involved. This was a measured, beautifully paced exhibition, with three sheep as placid as Rough Fells are ever likely to be.

The very next man has drawn a group which turns out to include a real trouble maker, who is reluctant to stay with the other two as they are brought down from the starting point, and then obstinately goes outside the pair of hurdles. The dog moves to fetch the miscreant, who unexpectedly turns and squares up. The unfortunate dog is at first nonplussed, and there is no shepherd's command to deal with a situation like this; but his professional reputation, his confidence even, is at stake. Dog and sheep remain motionless - dog on its belly, sheep stamping the ground with its foreleg. At length the dog's superior will-power wins the day. The sheep backs off slowly, but still refuses to join the other two. By now the shepherd's time is up but, as a final gesture, the dog brings the "awkward beggar" through the gate, and then goes off to fetch the other two.

No amount of training can allow for a situation like that but, on the fell, with the shepherd often out of sight and hearing, a dog has to improvise and use his judgement. So training is aimed not just at learning to obey commands, but at building up self-confidence and sound judgement. A shepherd will try to keep a measure of continuity, bringing on an apprentice as one of his other dogs is ageing. The time to start depends on the temperament of the young dog - usually between a year and eighteen months. Then he will find time to run this dog by itself, so that it will not pick up mannerisms from its elders. Many shepherds prefer to establish the essential mutual understanding between

Kentmere potter putting the finishing touches to a superb vase for pot-pourri

man and dog by means of whistled signals. This is on the whole quieter than verbal commands and, especially in formal trials, more likely to preserve that atmosphere of calm, in the absence of which everything is likely to go wrong. The best routine for training a young dog is to give him (or her) a few minutes each day after normal work is over, beginning with the simplest commands; lavish praise and the feeling that he is receiving special consideration will help the dog to enjoy his training, and look forward to carrying out increasingly complicated instructions.

Once trained, a dog can expect a working life of eight to ten years, with a peak between the ages of five and eight. Thereafter, although the skill developed through experience remains, the stamina for long runs over rough fell country begins to fail. This normal work is what keeps both shepherd and dog in training and creates the understanding that seems uncanny to an outsider. The exhibition work of trialling is simply everyday work polished to perfection in every respect. Some of the men at the trials have been out from an early hour, leaving everything in order at home before setting out. It is not yet eleven o'clock; two of them are standing silently watching, crook in hand, dogs lying unobtrusively at their feet. Their turn will not come until later in the day. After a while, one pushes his cap to the back of his head, and opens a conversation: "Have ye got yer baggin' 'Erb?" Things haven't really changed since Canon Rawnsley described these trials in 1902: *the critics take their pipes, and wait till the flag falls again, and another collie tries his luck... There is a pause for lunch. The shepherds and their dogs have been on the stretch since 9 o'clock; and there is a 'gay deal' of ginger ale popped off, and cups of tea, and slices of ham and bread are vigorously consumed at the refreshment tent."*

Before continuing down to Staveley, the pedestrian should take the short path to the dramatic falls where the River Kent has cut through the rocky barrier separating the upper from the lower valley. Baddeley was unkind enough to dismiss the lower section of Kentmere as "featureless", and no doubt the loss of its lake had diminished its beauty. This piece of environmental vandalism was perpetrated by over-zealous improvers early in the nineteenth century, when agricultural 'improvement' was in fashion. The shallow lake was drained in the largely mistaken expectation of creating a new area of potentially fertile land. Nevertheless, we who have not known the lake do not miss it, and it is still pleasant to walk through this narrow stretch of Kentmere vale, seldom more than two reasonably level fields in breadth, old ash trees marking out the lines of the moss-covered walls.

A person with a taste for such things could spend a long time in this valley looking for the traces of ancient settlements, which are dotted along its whole length, mostly on the higher ground. There would be no shortage of fish for the Neolithic or Iron Age inhabitants, even if the presence of wild boars in the woods made the trek to the river in search of salmon a trifle hazardous. At Staveley, by the mill lodge next to the road there is a fine salmon ladder to help them on their way even in these less abundant days. Now that it has been relieved of the continual stream of road traffic moving through its centre, Staveley has become once again a very pleasant little town but we are now outside the Lake District. To reach our last major valley, the best way would be to go back to Kentmere church, then cross Garburn Pass and, resolutely putting aside the attractions of Troutbeck for another time, to press on through Windermere to Bowness.

River Kent

Heading for a lake steamer

XII: Windermere

Now the sunlight catches the surface of a small shining tract far to the left; in half a minute more, you see another shining glimpse under the wooded banks of Heald Brow; and then you draw breath at the station, full in the narrow valley, and Windermere, the first of the lakes, lies like a dream of Eden at your feet.

Mrs Linton.

WINDERMERE and Bowness are really quite distinct towns, although nowadays equally dedicated to the tourist industry. Birthwaite was the name of the little settlement below Orrest Head, to which the railway company brought what turned out to be the terminus of its line from Kendal. This was not a name to excite the imagination of prospective visitors, so Birthwaite was rechristened Windermere. The expansion generated by the arrival of the railway in 1847 continued until the new railway town had joined up with the older holiday resort down by the lake. Along with Keswick, Bowness was one of the first places to be invaded by visitors. This was partly due to its position at the southern end of the main spinal road through the Lake District, and partly also to the sheer beauty of its situation.

There are frequent laments that the pressure of visitor numbers accompanied by the efforts of local entrepreneurs to cater for the wants of these people has wrecked whatever ambience survived the railway expansion. Yet if we look back 150 years, the impression we get is not one of calm and tranquil meditation; rather of a bustle and animation that is entirely recognisable. Windermere has always been the magnet for those who like

Bowness on Windermere; tourists sitting in the sun!

"messing about in boats". Many of the famous ones are now gathered in the Steamboat Museum near Bowness, where they hold regattas for model boat enthusiasts as well. The *Mannex* directory of 1847 homed in on the boats as the principal attraction: *Grand Annual Regattas are held here, and are attended by many of the families of distinction, and the inhabitants of the district, extending several miles round the lake, which on these festive days is crowded with boats and elegant barges, forming splendid aquatic processions attended by bands of music, and filled with gay and mirthful parties.* The spirit of Pocklington lived on! And Harriet Martineau, who had been established in Ambleside for ten years when she wrote her *Guide to the Lakes* in 1855, writes in a similar vein, with a very contemporary warning about safety on the lake. (At Bowness): *the steamboats put up, and thence go forth the large number of fishing and pleasure boats by which the lake is adorned... What a crowd of boatmen, boats, jetties, omnibuses, yelling steam yachts and visitors of all grades, we suddenly come upon in that little bay.* But continues Harriet, anyone who goes sailing should be accompanied by *a person who understands the management of sailing boats.*

If today the continuing presence of *visitors of all grades* strikes a jarring note, then choose a winter morning, not necessarily a sunny one, to look across the water from one of those jetties. The chances are that your only company will be the ducks, bobbing up and down on the wavelets; the woods on the farther shore will be half hidden by mists, so that there is no telling what dangerous crags or haunted glades they may conceal - the same prospect, in fact, that had reduced the poet Gray to a nervous wreck at the thought of having to cross in order to continue his journey.

It is easy enough to cross now, by the large ferry boat. All those people who sit resolutely inside their cars pass up the opportunity to enjoy the view in every direction, but especially north beyond Belle Isle to the rugged mountain line. The ferry trip enables us to go and look at a unique survival from the early years of Windermere's popularity - Claife Station, in the woods just above Ferry House and the road running on to Sawrey and Hawkshead. This building, now in the care of the National Trust, has nothing to do with the railway company, but is a viewing station. A carefully constructed path, of easy gradient and wide enough for a pony and trap, winds up the hillside, and brings us to a large building two storeys high. It is an impressive structure, of good quality stone with a castellated roof. The ground floor was a dining room; and an elegantly curved flight of stone steps gives access to the upper room, lit by large windows and looking towards the lake. Trees have now grown tall around and below, thereby obscuring the view and hiding the building itself which, when Harriet Martineau wrote her 'Guide', was the most celebrated tourist landmark along the entire length of Windermere.

The explanation is to be found in the earliest, and most influential, of all Lake District 'Guides' - that of Thomas West, published in 1778. He advised visitors to stop at what he considered to be the best viewpoints, so that they could admire the prospect. Claife was the first of five 'stations' in the circuit of Windermere. The idea was to stand and look through your landscape mirror. *These,* explained West, *are of plano-convex glass of four to four and a half inches in diameter, and should be the segment of a large circle; otherwise, distant and small objects are not perceived in them.* A person using the glass had to turn his back on the object under scrutiny, holding the mirror by the upper part of its case. Then, by looking into the glass, *objects great and near are removed to a due distance, shewn in the soft colours of nature, and in the most regular perspective the eye can perceive.* This doesn't seem

Bathing pool; model makers putting their creations through trials

very different from taking a car mirror round with you!

However, by the 1790s the station building had been constructed for the greater comfort of visitors. From the upper room it was possible to look at West's view. Baddeley was a bit supercilious about it: *by the aid of coloured glass, the visitor is supposed to be able to transport himself into whichever season of the year best pleases him.* Wordsworth had been no more enthusiastic: *The view from the Pleasure-house of the Station near the Ferry has suffered much from larch plantations.* He didn't like larches, of course, so that didn't help. But probably most of the folk who came across for a romantic candle-lit dinner dance weren't all that bothered about the view, anyway.

Back in Bowness, and before taking the steamer to the foot of the lake (much the most satisfactory way of getting there), the discerning visitor should try to look inside Saint Martin's Church, one of the finest and biggest in the Lake District. Quite apart from the quality of the architecture, it contains a quantity of superb stained glass, dating from the fifteenth century and earlier, and a number of beautifully preserved inscriptions on the walls. These are in the form of question and answer, and were clearly put there for the edification of parishioners soon after the Reformation settlement - probably in the late sixteenth century - so as to divert them from any lingering influence of Popery. Thus: *Is the breade and wine turned into the boddie and bloode of Christ: NO.* That they were staunch upholders of Protestantism here is further illustrated by the secular inscription composed by a local gentleman, Christopher Philipson, in 1629 to celebrate the failure of the Gunpowder Plot, a quarter of a century earlier. A more easily comprehensible, and less controversial memorial in the church is to Lakeland's best guide, Baddeley.

At this point, he (Baddeley, that is) would pack us off to Lakeside on the steamer, so as to get the best view of the wooded hills that enfold the lower basin of the lake. At Lakeside we are in touch with the railway again, if only for the short distance down the Leven Valley to Haverthwaite/Backbarrow. This is the heartland of the old industrial Lakeland, where there are relics of just about every industry which once took advantage of the almost unlimited supplies of wood and water power.

Having come from Bowness without any effort at all, we can quite easily walk up through Backbarrow village, to a vantage point at High Brow Edge above Low Wood. Down at Haverthwaite, the terminus of this fragment of the old line to Lakeside, a steam engine hoots. It is hidden by the trees, but soon the clouds of smoke come out into the open as a little saddle-tank engine pulling five coaches works noisily, wearily, up the steep gradient. Slowly, it winds out of sight into the woodland, taking another cargo of visitors to Lakeside. The tourist industry now dominates the Leven Valley. Some of the rail passengers may have been staying in the vast 'Lakeland Village' which has transformed the site of the old 'dolly blue' works.

The main factory building has been adapted to become part of the village - at least its third transformation because in the early days of the Industrial Revolution it was a cotton mill, just like the ones in Preston or Bolton. It was notorious for the way in which the pauper children, imported from far away, were grievously ill-treated. Backbarrow has been a working rather than a picture-book village all its life, and for that reason seldom rates more than a passing mention in the older guides. Industry was not confined to the factory. Only a few yards downstream is the site of the ironworks, one of the biggest in the north of England for the best part of two centuries. Then, looking down over Low Wood, is the

Train leaves Haverthwaite bound for Lakeside

clock tower which marks the former gunpowder works. The industrial archaeologist could happily spend an entire holiday in this valley, and, moreover, spend it amid the most delightful woodland surroundings. The charcoal that was produced in the Furness woods provides the key to the presence of these industries, and also reminds us that the woods themselves were not decorative in intention, but strictly utilitarian and housed many industries of their own. It is not difficult to find the circular platforms known as pitsteads, where the charcoal burners worked. The woods, mainly hazel and oak, were cut as coppice every fifteen to twenty years, so that the poles could be used primarily by the 'coalers'. When the trees have been cut like this, almost to ground level, they send up a whole lot of new poles from the stool, which means that the woodland resources were self-renewing.

The charcoal burners were not the only ones interested in the wood, of course. For centuries local craftsmen made hoops, or barrels, or turned dishes on their lathes and, at the time when the cotton mill was flourishing, bobbins. For much of the nineteenth century, bobbin making was a boom industry, and there were scores of bobbin mills throughout the Lake District, particularly in Furness. At Stott Park, not far from Lakeside, one of the last to remain in business has been rescued by the Planning Board and restored to working order. Here one may see not only how the bobbins were made, but also appreciate that the children at the cotton mill were not the only ones to get a raw deal from life. Much of the work must have been suffocatingly tedious, carried out in squalid conditions amid unguarded machinery and unprotected belting.

Most of the woodland industries, having for so long helped to created the lowland landscape that looks so beautiful from Brow Edge, have been made obsolete by developments in technology, and changing industrial patterns. A few have clung to life - like bark-peeling. In spring, when the sap was rising, the bark peelers took their sharp knives to the oak poles that were to be cut later in the year, and deftly stripped away the bark. Then it was taken to one or other of the many local tanneries. There was one in nearly every village, and, in the Rusland Valley, and not far from here, the Planning Board has succeeded in preserving, though not in operating, as it does the Stott Park bobbin mill, a virtually complete tannery. The market for bark is now very limited indeed, but it still exists, and in certain retired corners of Furness it is possible to see bundles of bark, neatly tied with baler twine, piled by the wayside awaiting collection. Another old industry which refuses to die, and is even experiencing a modest revival because its products are attractive-looking, hard-wearing and useful, is besom making. Nothing sweeps a yard or a lawn better than a well tied bundle of birch twigs!

But the industry which has re-established itself most firmly through south Lakeland has been that of swill basket making. Not many years ago, it looked as if this craft would die with the old men - several resident in this valley - who practised it. There was no longer any demand for shallow open baskets which lines of sweating workmen could carry to refill the coal bunker of ocean-going ships; no-one wanted baskets, shaped to fit round one hip, to hold seed corn when sowing by hand; Scottish potato picking had been mechanised; butchers no longer wanted big baskets for taking round their deliveries; grocers and feed merchants no longer used scuttles, wide at one end and tapering, for filling sacks... Then the industry which created the Lakeland Village, and sustains the economy of the Leven Valley today, came to the rescue. These baskets have many uses around the home, and are not readily available in Wolverhampton or Milton Keynes - they will hold logs by the fire,

Mike turns a bobbin at Stott Park Bobbin Mill (an English Heritage Estate)

or some of the children's toys, or materials in the garden; so why not take one back at the end of the holiday?

The result is that swillers are back in business. It is a difficult craft to learn, but one which must give great satisfaction to the craftsman. He uses the oak poles, of about six inches diameter, that the bark peeler has peeled, storing them in a big, airy shed until the next winter. Wood that is ready for use is cut into workable lengths of about three feet, then quartered by splitting. These pieces are put to soak in a big iron water trough - maybe seven feet long and eighteen inches wide. Above the trough is a canopy to extract the steam, and underneath a flue along its whole length - because, next day, you get a fire going in your furnace to boil all this wood, in order to soften it. When the water has cooled enough to allow you to handle the pieces, you reach them out one at a time, literally to tear them apart into long, thin strips, after making an incision with a sharp knife at one end. To do this, you need a pad to protect your knees, and hands made strong by working long years at the craft. By the time the trough is cleared, you will be knee-deep in oak strips, ready to be smoothed to make the interwoven body of the basket.

The oval basket rim, or bool, is made of hazel, to which the smoothed oak strips known as tars will have to be fixed. The smoothing has been done on the craftsman's 'mare'. You sit on one end of this long wooden contraption, then you fix the tar in front of you by applying pressure on a foot pedal which brings down a big wooden brake onto the tar. All is now ready to dress and shape the tar with your drawknife, a sort of enlarged spokeshave, which you pull towards yourself, using both hands. And so on, until you have done sufficient tars in varying widths. Now comes the really difficult part of the job; fastening the strips to the rim.

The vital strip is the first one - the lapping spell, which is the central crosspiece along the shorter axis. The depth of the basket is determined by the length of this first spell, so before it is tied to the rim by means of narrow strips, you run a wooden measuring stick round it, just to make sure your practiced eye hasn't deceived you. Strength of finger and wrist as well as dexterity is involved now, as four more crosswise spells are fixed before putting in the first of the longer strips, going alternately over and under. When the body of the basket has been finished, the whole thing is held together largely by the inter-related stresses created by its own construction - a perfect example of functional design; easy to handle, light in weight, simple in shape. The most serious problem facing those who have revived the craft is in obtaining the wood, because for so many years the oak coppices have been neglected, and they take about twenty-five years to grow again from scratch.

Looking away from the busy woodlands, the view extends over the estuary of the River Leven, which very soon enters the sea at Greenodd, meeting the Crake from Coniston Water as it does so. The water lying on the distant sands glitters in the sunlight; Black Combe, in the far distance, is cloud-capped even on this sunny day. Its industries always militated against Backbarrow becoming popular or fashionable, but times have changed, and there can be few better centres for exploring the low hills and deciduous woodlands of the southern Lake District. One of the joys is to find the secret paths and little byroads along which it is possible to walk back beside, or not far from the western shore of Windermere to Ferry House, and so across the lake to Bowness again.

The laziest way of getting to Ambleside would have been to take the 'steamer' all the way from Lakeside, but unless the day is very hot, or very wet, it is more rewarding to walk

Right:
Backbarrow iron
furnace, hearth stone

Left:
Hayes' modernistic
greenhouse,
Ambleside

from the ferry through Bowness and up to Orrest Head. This famous viewpoint is easily reached by a clearly marked path, and fully justifies the reputation it has always had. After a rest on one of the seats thoughtfully placed near the summit, more careful navigation is needed. Footpaths take us through the fields, by Near and Far Orrest, down in the direction of Troutbeck. This is unspoiled 'old Westmorland' countryside, relatively quiet even in the busy holiday season. Then, having climbed up on the other side of the Troutbeck valley, the path continues through farmyards and woodland, high above the lake, right into Ambleside. This way roughly follows the line of the ancient Roman road to the fort at Borrans near the head of Windermere. There are no crowds up here, and the changing vista over the lake to the line of mountains dominated by the Langdale Pikes is a continual delight. Jenkin Crag is a good place to stop for a while, and reflect that we have almost completed our journey up and down the 'spokes' of the Lake District 'wheel'. To reach our starting point we need only walk the short stage back to Grasmere through Rydal.

But there is still much to detain us on the way, not least in Ambleside itself, squeezed into the narrow space that the Rothay has cut into the mountains. The town stands in much the same relationship to its lake as Keswick does to Derwentwater, but is more immediately hemmed in by the surrounding fells. Like Keswick too, it had been a place of local importance for centuries before the first visitors arrived, and it has kept a strong sense of community, though struggling to preserve its individual character. When the name of the old inn that had always been known as the 'Salutation' was changed some years ago to the 'Royal Yachtsman', there was such an outcry that the original name had to be reinstated. And Ambleside is always a force to be reckoned with in the Westmorland cricket and football leagues. Members of the teams are fortunate to be able to play in such wonderful surroundings - the footballers 'laike' in Millans Park, the cricketers out on the Rydal road, opposite the parkland where the sheepdog trials and the sports take place.

In the Lakeland calendar, Ambleside Sports vies with Grasmere for pre-eminence, both as an attraction for thousands of visitors, and a magnet to local enthusiasts. The events are varied and the standards are high, but there is no doubt that what principally draws the crowds is the senior guides race. Like Cumberland and Westmorland wrestling, fell racing is a sport particularly linked with the Lake District. Rydal Park is an ideal venue, because Low Fell makes a perfect course - not oppressively high, and not so far away that the spectators cannot see what is going on. The runners in the senior race have probably served an apprenticeship as competitors in the junior races when they were in their teens, and they will certainly have been training systematically for the summer programme. In their home villages, neighbours will have seen them in the early morning before work, or in the evenings, clocking seventy to eighty miles a week of basic running. They vary this with the specialist training needed for the fells - speed runs or downhill plunges.

The fell runner has to be master of many techniques. He must be able to sprint, so that he can move clear of the field at the start, or bring out that little bit extra on the final stretch in a neck and neck finish; he has to be capable of the endurance of the long-distance man, in that heart-punishing uphill slog; he needs to cultivate the balance and agility of a mountain goat for rushing downhill; and, above all, the skill to adapt his style to all kinds of terrain - short grass on bumpy ground, long tussocky grass, stony slopes, boggy areas, places where in running obliquely along a hillside one foot is at a lower level than the

Waterhead, Windermere

other...

And so we hear the steward ring his bell, and call through the loudspeaker: "Will the competitors for the senior fell race assemble in the enclosure," and at this point even the diehards totter out of the beer tent. There will be about a dozen men, some nervously jumping up and down or slapping their calf muscles, all wearing brightly coloured vests and shorts and shoes with special lethal-looking spikes. Off they go at the sound of the starter's gun, sprinting across the damp field, jockeying for a good position to get over the wall or gate without being hampered by any rivals. There may be several gates in this first, relatively level stretch of a run, making it rather like a steeplechase. By the time the real fellside is reached, one or two runners will have drawn away from the field. The going gets harder now; the gradient is more severe, the ground rougher. Up, up the steepening hillside, trying to preserve the rhythm of running for as long as possible, although inevitably the pace has slowed to walking speed. Nearing the flag at the climax of the run, the leading man glances back. If his nearest rival is twenty yards behind, he is as good as home, because in the time it will take to cover those last few paces, he himself will have plunged a hundred yards or more back downhill and established an impregnable psychological advantage.

This is the most exciting part of the run, as the competitors leap down in giant strides, just within the limit of keeping physical control of their limbs, arms often stretched out wide, eyes on the ground ahead. It is easy to fall if a shoe catches the edge of a stone, almost impossible to see in the bracken cover. Yet somehow they usually all stay upright, fighting their private battles for supremacy as they see they have no chance of keeping up with the leaders, who are even now scrambling over the final walls and receiving the congratulations of the crowd.

Why do they do it? The answer usually is that they love running up and down these fellsides, astonishing as this may seem to those of us who could scarcely scramble to the top of, say, one of those dreadful gullies on the Coniston run, even on our hands and knees. Another answer would be that they do it because this is a genuine traditional local activity. Records of the Grasmere Sports go back to the middle of the nineteenth century, but the origins of fell racing, like those of wrestling, are lost in folk memory. They used to have games at weddings and funerals in the dales, rather as the ancient Etruscans did; contests involving physical skill and prowess have always been an attraction to the dalesman. When a shepherd or a foxhunter today wants to get up a hillside quickly for what to him is an urgent and practical reason, he will leave most of the visiting hikers standing at the post. Let it be understood that he must have a reason for wanting to climb quickly; he would not normally dream of doing it for fun. But in the old days, when there were fewer distractions in August, with the ewes back on the fell, haytiming over, and the hunting season not begun, it is not farfetched to see the younger men adding a fell race to the idle distractions of a summer afternoon.

Wordsworth's last home, Rydal Mount, looks down to the parkland where we have been enjoying the sports. We are now back in the same valley where we began in Chapter I, only on the other side of the river. We have no need to follow the main road back to Grasmere, except that there is no better viewpoint for appreciating the delicate beauty of Rydal Water. Then we can take the old route from White Moss, over the shoulder of the common, and down to Dove Cottage. Wordsworth walked here often, and in his verse

Boat mooring and reeds, Windermere

celebrated individual rocks and trees for their associations with one or other of his family or friends, or for some eccentricity in their shape or appearance.

On a calm, grey winter day we too can take delight in the details of the scene: a solitary bird is cheeping somewhere among the hazels that are loaded with next year's catkins, waiting tightly closed for the first breath of spring in January. Looking higher up for our bird, we become aware of the filigree patterns made by the birch trees against the uniform grey of the sky. A little farther on, Grasmere comes into sight through the trees; in its still water Loughrigg Terrace and Silver Howe lie reflected. From the top of the road, Grasmere village beyond the silent fields merges indistinctly with the more distant landscape towards Helm Crag.

More than anyone else, perhaps, Wordsworth has taught us to see the Lake District in the fine detail of its trees and flowers, as well as in the majestic sweep of valley and fell. He taught us also that we are the guardians of it, a lesson not lost on John Ruskin who, in turn, warned vehemently and eloquently against accepting every specious plan for 'development'. In a letter of 1884, for example, to the *Manchester City News*, he gave full rein to his imagination: *It is easy to conceive...a High Street of magnificent establishments of millinery and 'nouveautés' running along under the hills from Ambleside to Grasmere, with the railway to Keswick immediately in their rear.* (This was one of his 'anti-railway-in-the-wrong-place' letters.) *I behold the sublimity of Wordsworth Crescent and Silver How Circus, commanding the esplanade which will encompass the waters of Rydal and Grasmere, principally then, of necessity, composed of sewage...* Not too wide of the mark when we consider Bowness and Windermere a century later, and a very sobering thought that ours is the responsibility to ensure that these Lake District valleys are still protected from the self-seeking pressures of commercial exploitation.

Typesetting and design by Carnmor Print & Design, London Road, Preston, Lancs, UK
Printed in Hong Kong by Vimnice Printing Press Co. Ltd

A Dream of Eden

When Mrs Lynn Linton wrote a guidebook to the Lake District in the last century she described the area as being 'a dream of Eden'. This book, illustrated by the stunning colour and monochrome pictures of David Briggs, shows the area has lost none of its charm today. Like Mrs Linton, John Dawson and David Briggs live in the area and know it intimately. The book concentrates on the valleys and the people who live there; John Dawson's text explaining frankly what life is like today. Is it still a dream of Eden?

For the visitor many local mysteries are solved - and especially those concerning the ever-present ubiquitous sheep. This book is an up-to-date companion guide to Britain's most popular tourist area.

JOHN DAWSON came to the Lake District in 1960 as Headmaster of the John Ruskin School, Coniston. As a student he had read History at Jesus College, Cambridge, so retirement in 1982 gave him the opportunity to pick up the threads of earlier studies. He has contributed the Lake District section to *Britain's National Parks* (Windward Books, 1984), compiled a detailed history of the *Lakeland parish of Torver* (Phillimore, 1985), written articles for many periodicals, particularly *Country Life, Lancashire Life* and *Cumbria,* often in collaboration with David Briggs, and written several historical monographs on subjects of local interest.

He is also Hon. Curator of the Ruskin Museum, Coniston, and has lectured on John Ruskin and subjects associated with the history of the Lake District. He and his wife, Margaret, still live at Coniston, despite its 100 inches of rain each year, because they cannot imagine anywhere better!

DAVID BRIGGS ARPS lives in the Furness area of South Lakeland and is employed by Vickers Shipbuilding & Engineering, Barrow-in-Furness as a manager.

He has had a long interest in photography and is an Associate of the Royal Photographic Society. His photographs have been exhibited throughout Cumbria and especially at the Brewery Arts Centre, Kendal, and Furness Galleries, Ulverston. His photographic interests range between portraiture and pictorial landscape and his work appears regularly in magazines such as Country Life to which he and John Dawson have contributed for many years. Together they also produced *Wordsworth's Duddon Revisited* (Cicerone).

David Briggs, with his wife Jill and daughters Sarah and Jenny, lives in Penny Bridge, a small village in the Crake Valley.

CICERONE
MILNTHORPE CUMBRIA

ISBN 1-85284-104-4

9 781852 841041